Roberto Luciani

THE COLOSSEUM

Architecture, history and entertainment in the Flavian amphitheatre, ancient Rome's most famous building

ISTITUTO GEOGRAFICO
DeAGOSTINI

Editor-in-Chief: Marcella Boroli

Staff Editor: Pieranna Pagan

Editorial staff: Silvia Broggi, Cristina Drago

Editorial secretary: Maria Pia Arciuli

Translators: Alberto Gabba and George Mc Claud Meredith

Revision and Editing: Rossella Carpinella

Graphic design: Otello Geddo

Lay-out: Ennio Rancati

Photographic research: Centro Iconografico dell'Istituto
Geografico De Agostini

Page 1: A gilded bronze sesterce minted on the orders of the Senate after the death of Titus in 81 A.D.

Page 2: An aerial photograph of the Colosseum.

Catalogue 25485
ISBN 88-405-0827-5

Printed in Italy — Officine Grafiche De Agostini, Novara, 1990

CONTENTS

THE ORIGINS

The morphological configuration of the hollow between the Oppius hills to the North, the Palatine to the South-West, the Celius to the South and the Velia to the North-West, and its own marshy nature due mostly to its being crossed by the Labicanus brook flowing southwards from Lateranus and towards the Circus Maximus, certainly did not favour human settlement in what was later to be known as the 'Colosseum Valley'. During the Republican period the area was occupied by modest private houses and by some warehouses (*horrea*), which had gained building space as a result of partial draining of the surface waters and raising the ground by means of embankments. Under Augustus (27 B.C. - 14 A.D.) the whole area was included in the III urban region called *Isis et Serapis* and was chosen as the site for the first permanent amphitheatre in Rome. Yet the Augustan project was soon abandoned and the valley kept its swamps for many years.
With the Emperor Nero, the whole area acquired a new appearance thanks to the prince's urban-planning programme; he saw the renovative, messianic nature of his own reign showing itself even in the extension of the town to places traditionally uninhabited or only partially exploited.

Already in the very first year of his reign (54 A.D.) the youthful Nero had built, on the slope of Mount Celius towards the valley, a large temple in honour of Claudius, his adoptive father and predecessor, thus opening the way to the extension of monument building also to the south-eastern part of the city, which was still in private hands. In 60 A.D. Nero started to enlarge the imperial palaces, the *Domus Transitoria*, a series of buildings which had to unite the imperial residences on the Palatine with the *Horti* (gardens) on the Esquiline. It was the great fire of 64 A.D., however, which offered Nero an excellent opportunity for total urban renewal. In only five days, ten of the fourteen districts into which Augustus had divided the town were destroyed, losing for ever hundreds of works of art of the imperial collections. After the fire Nero took vigorous measures to provide for

the reconstruction of the districts, adopting preventive methods against possible future fires. Even more admirable was the reconstruction of a new great imperial palace, which had to exceed in size all royal residences of antiquity, the *Domus Aurea* (Golden House).
The historian Suetonius (*Nero* 39 A.D.) satirizes the extent of Nero's new home, saying that it was so huge that the city itself seemed but a part of it. Indeed the new residence convulsed the city, which, as a consequence, adapted itself to a new plan, including wider streets lined with arcades and new districts of a characteristic regularity. The extension of the great imperial villa is still a controversial topic; yet the testimonies of some ancient authors and the few archaeological remains at our disposal can give us an idea, albeit approximative, of its articulation. The poet Martial affirms

that the palace occupied the area extending from Mount Celius, where the temple of Claudius had been transformed into a large nymphaeum, to the Palatine; then, along the ridge of the Velia it joined with the Oppius, embracing all the great Esquiline gardens.
The whole extension was around 80 hectares, equivalent to one quarter of the whole surface area then occupied by Rome.

Above: a first century bronze bust of the Emperor Nero. The bust comes from Cilicia, in present day Turkey. The Louvre, Paris. Left: a neoclassical print by G. Chedanne which offers an imaginative reconstruction of the Domus Aurea's Hall of Laocoön. Musée des Beaux-Arts, Rouen.

Opposite page: a detail of the decorations in the Domus Aurea, or 'Golden House'. This was a group of imperial palaces built by Nero on the site later occupied by the Colosseum.

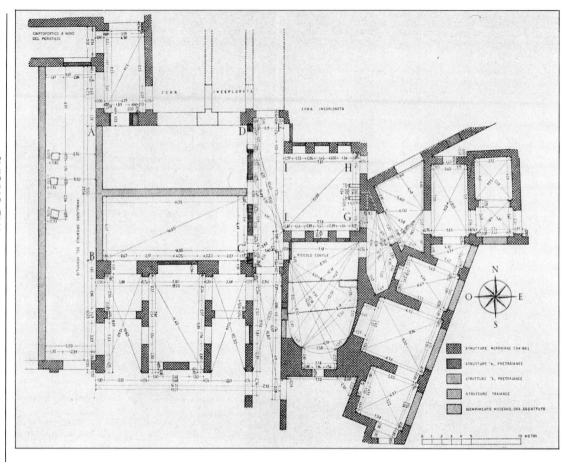

The palace proper was inserted in an artificial terrace on the Oppius, with only one frontage, which looked southwards, while the enormous entrance opened with a porch onto the Velia. In the atrium on the Velia, Nero had placed a statue representing himself dressed as the Sun God, a good 70 cubits (about 32 metres) high, cast in bronze by Zenodoros. Yet the real centre of the Neronian palace was established in the deep valley of the Labicanus brook, which Nero had controlled and drained into a small lake, surrounded by monumental pavilions and used at opportune moments for the performance of naval battles (*naumachiae*). The most recent excavations carried out on the Colosseum side have brought to light some Neronian sites belonging to the *Domus Aurea* pavilions near the little lake. These were long porticoes, crowned by rooms probably more adapted to service functions than to habitations. The Neronian villa remained in use after Nero's death, under his successor Oto, but one year later it had already been partially demolished by the first of the Flavii.

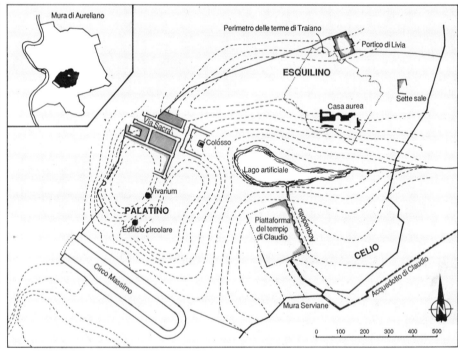

Top of the page: a map of the Domus Aurea with the two parts of the villa dating back to different periods, as the shape of the rooms very clearly shows.
Above: the park surrounding Nero's residence. From L. Benevolo's History of the City.

Opposite page: a first century mural depicting a stretch of water surrounded by imposing architecture. The setting is not unlike that of the Domus Aurea. Museo Archeologico Nazionale, Naples.

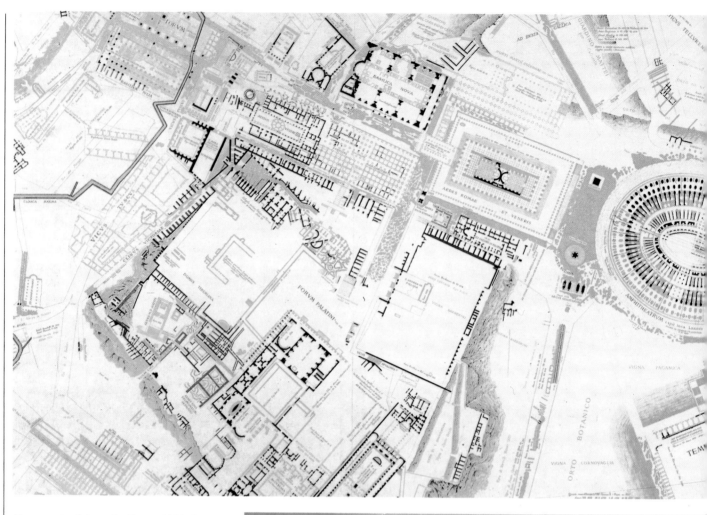

Above: a detail from the Forma Urbis Romae Antiquae, *the first monumental map of ancient Rome. The map was drafted between 1893 and 1901 by Rodolfo Lanciani, who worked from a plan that had been carved in marble during the Severian period. This detail shows the area around the Colosseum.*

Right: the Colosseum and, on the opposite page, an architectural model of the monument; three floors of arches, stressed by semicolumned pillars of Tuscan, Ionic and Corinthian order, rise over a two-stepped stylobate. The structure is crowned by an attic which is decorated with a combination of rectangular windows and gilded bronze shields.

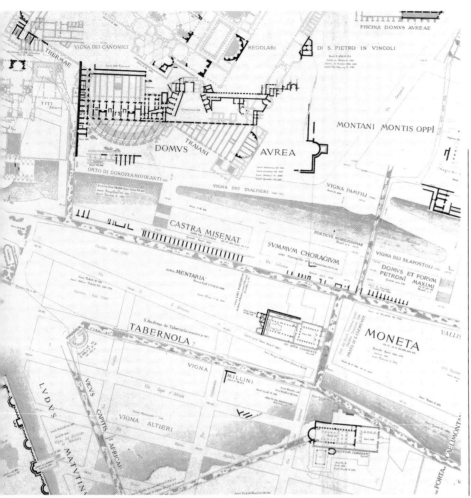

THE FLAVII

Nero's politicies hurt the interests of the senatorial class and compromised his own control over provincial activities. Thus the last years of Nero's reign were characterized by rebellions in the provinces and after his death it was the old senator Sulpicius Galba who rose to power.

The election of one of the most obvious representatives of the senatorial aristocracy was, however, a cause for discontent, especially amongst the praetorian cohorts, who after a few months elected Marcus Salvius Oto as the new emperor. Almost at the same time the legions which were fighting on the Rhine front elected prince

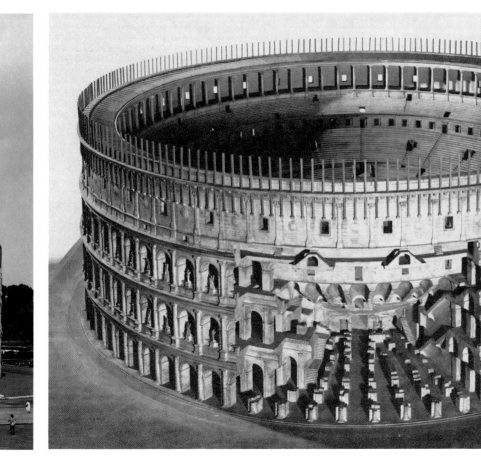

Below: a section of the Colosseum's main
axis and the surrounding area,
as far as the Temple of Venus and Rome.

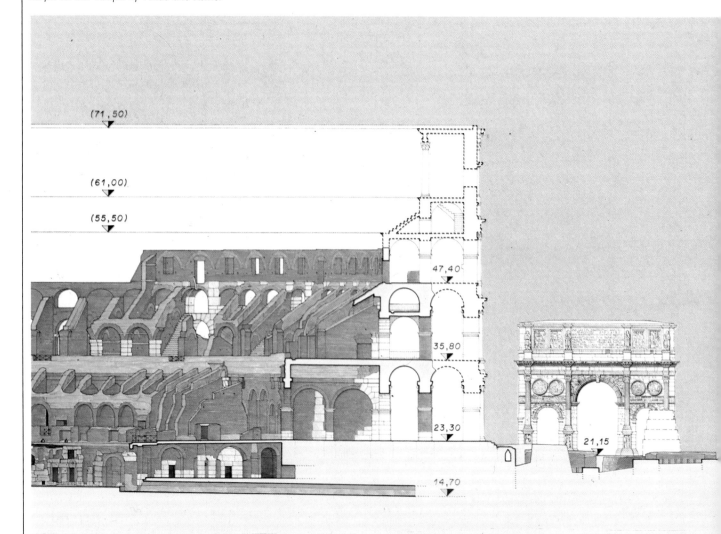

Opposite page: a reconstruction, made by Cyro Nispi-Landi at the beginning of this century, of the Flavian Ampitheatre and the famous statue of Colossus. It is believed that they were originally built in the fifth century. According to one theory, ornamental statues were placed in the barrel-vaults of the arches.

Below: the front towards the Colosseum of the Temple of Venus and Rome, together with Massenzio's Basilica, the statue of Colossus and the Meta Sudans, as seen by Ernest Georges Coquart in 1863. L'Ecole Nationale Supérieure des Beaux-Arts, Paris.

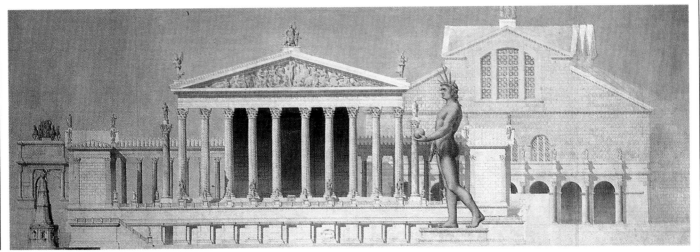

their general Aulus Vitellius, while those engaged in the Middle East elected their commander Flavius Vespasian. The imperial power struggle between these three personalities characterized the rest of 68 A.D. and part of 69, a period that historians called *longus et unus annus*.

Flavius Vespasian emerged as the winner of these bloody clashes. A man of modest family origins, he held power for ten years and opened the way to the second imperial dynasty, that of the Flavii. Vespasian soon expressed the interests of the Italic middle classes, to the detriment of the rich landowning patricians.

The first blow to the aristocracy was given by the Emperor's strict ideal of refurnishing the public treasury, greatly impoverished by the high building expenses of the Neronian period and by civil disorders. Nevertheless, he continued the Neronian plan in part, reconstructing all those town areas which had remained free from buildings after the fires and the collapses. Very important in this respect was the purpose reserved for all those sites previously occupied by Nero's grand 'Golden House' and by its pavilions and gardens, restored to the state by Vespasian with his promise that they should be devoted soon after to public amusement. This urban planning intervention was therefore a real change of position towards the monument building and administrative operations of the former principalities, particularly those of the Neronian era, as if to point out that the new ways had definitively abolished the gap existing between the mass of the people and the luxury and unbridled amusement of the court.

A direct consequence of this policy was the construction of great public buildings for the benefit of the people, like the Temple of Peace which opened up again the arguments about forum squares and, above all, the Flavian Amphitheatre. Some repair or partial reconstruction of existing buildings was also carried out, such as the restitution of the large Neronian Nymphaeum on the Celius to the cult of the divine Claudius, the restoration of the Venus of Coo and the imposing one of Nero's Colossus on the Velia. But Vespasian greatest work surely was the huge amphitheatre, even if the merit of its inauguration fell to his son Titus, who succeeded the day after his father's death in 79 A.D.

Titus'reign lasted only three years, but was characterized by intense political, military and social activity which carried the Emperor to the highest levels of popular esteem and love (he was nicknamed by the people 'the delight of mankind'). Even in his short reign Titus had time to complete many of his father's enterprises including the Colosseum itself, which he solemnly inaugurated with one hundred days of shows and feasts in the summer of 80 A.D. The amphitheatre was thus opened for public amusement with great celebrations involving all the entertainment houses in the city, even the oldest and most uncomfortable such as the old Augustan Naumachia beyond the Tiber which had not been used for years. For the same occasion a special coinage of sesterces was struck, figuring the amphitheatre on the reverse, and all men of art and culture were set to work. Yet the Colosseum had still not assumed the appearance it was to have at the height of the imperial age; at the time of inauguration almost certainly both the hypogea underground and the scenic machinery that made it a wonder of scenographic technique were absent. Perhaps missing also was the *maenianum summum*, i.e. the wooden steps reserved for the female public, under the portico of the attic. It was Titus'successor, his brother Flavius Domitian, who took care of all these works and who reviewed and perfected the decorative apparatus.

Domitian ascent to power in 81 A.D. was for him an unhoped redemption.

Domitian was ten years younger than his brother, and he had always lived in his shadow. Titus had been his father's favourite, and had been more socially and politically active. The new Emperor tried to win the people's favour by means of food distributions and above all by organizing literary contests, gladiatorial and circus games. He had the Flavian Amphiteatre finished in all respects and several storage buildings were constructed in its immediate vicinity, with a view to perfecting efficiency.

Thus, with the addition of gladiatorial barracks and of warehouses, the whole Colosseum was finally complete.

Opposite page: a bas-relief from the tomb
of the Haterii showing the buildings of Flavian
Rome. The Colosseum is second from the left.
Musei Vaticani, Rome.

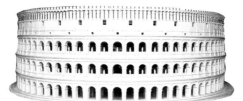

Left: an architectural model of the Flavian
Ampitheatre, made by Carlo Lucangeli in 1796
and currently housed in the Colosseum's
Antiquarium.
Below: a bird's eye view (by Braum and
Hogemberg in 1618) of the area surrounding
the ampitheatre. Biblioteca Marciana, Venice.

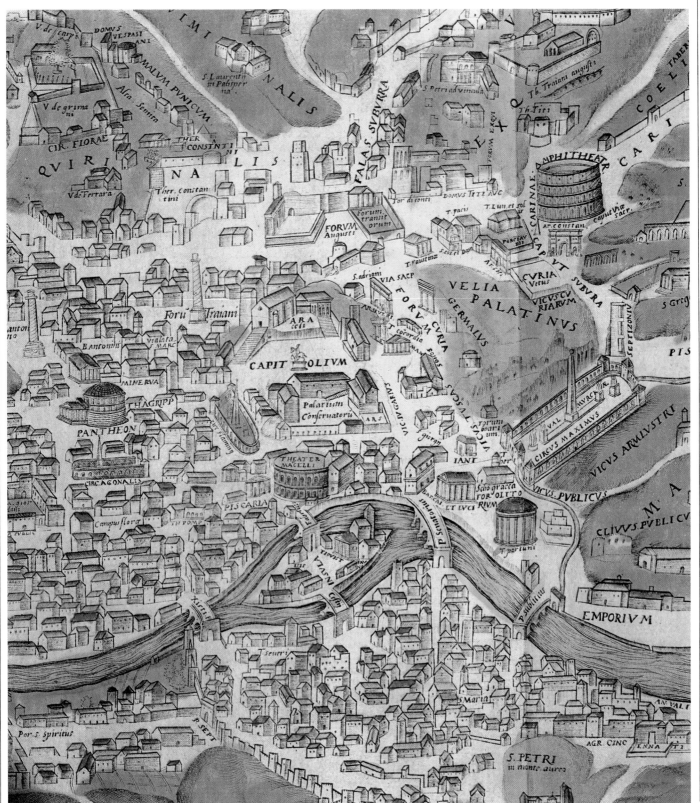

THE CONSTRUCTION

As opposed to other earlier Roman amphitheatres of wooden construction, the Colosseum had to give an impression of solidity and power, consecrating the ideological might of the Roman state by its very dimensions. The responsibility for its execution was entrusted to a person certainly ingenious, but unluckily bound to remain anonymous, since we do not find any reference to him in ancient sources, nor in any historical tradition. Some have wanted to recognize in the construction of the Colosseum the genius of Rabirius, the architect of Domitian and designer of the palace on the Palatine; others on the basis of a Christian epigraph coming from St. Agnes cemetery on Via Nomentana, have identified him as the Gaudentius killed by Vespasian himself because of his Christian faith; others again have seen in the great building the provincial style of a Germanic freeman. None of these hypotheses can be considered reliable and for this reason the name of the architect, together with the causes for the complete silence on the part of all sources, remains a mystery. In any case it is true that, with few exceptions, Roman architectural works are anonymous. This is because the designer was merely one of the many functionaries engaged in glorifying the Emperor.

In the case of the Colosseum, the anonymous architect did an excellent job, endowing Rome with a building of a type not yet present in the city. The amphitheatre, as an architectural type, was born in Campania in the last years of the Republic and had quickly won favour among the Italics, spreading into many towns of the peninsula in more or less monumental forms. Rome didn't have an amphitheatre until the age of Augustus, but the wooden construction, built by the entrepreneur Statilius Taurus in the Campus Martius, was actually temporary. Almost immediately Augustus had the idea of providing the city with a massive building, to be situated right in the Labicanus valley, between the Oppius and Velia hills.

The building of an amphitheatre responded to precise ideological and demagogic demands, and lent itself to the typical Roman custom of a performance with gladiatorial games (*ludi gladiatorii*) and animal hunts (*venationes*).

Nevertheless, as we have seen, it was only half a century later, with the advent of Flavian emperors, that the construction of the great amphitheatre was begun.

The amphitheatre of Rome, in order to fulfil its functional and ideological tasks, had not only to respect all the rules dictated by the typology, but also had to exceed in dimensions all similar buildings. Thus the huge building was elliptical in shape, the two external axes being 188 x 156 m with an arena analogous in shape whose axes were 87.30 x 54.30. The base of the cavea, or tiers of seats, was to be a constant 51 m, with a gradient of 37°, while the whole structure was to reach a height of 48.60 metres.

In order to build the Colosseum, it was necessary to supply various materials, above all travertine, tufa and bricks, and to keep more than a dozen groups of specialized labourers costantly at work. Travertine came from the great Tiber quarries, that had been specially linked to Rome by a straight road, 20 feet (about six metres) wide. This kind of expedient was necessary, if it is considered that in order to build the whole monument more than 100,000 cubic metres of travertine were cut in different dimensions and were given the finishing touch at the time they were put into position. Every block

Left: a detail from the second and third order of the external arcades.
Below: a detail of the internal arcades. The architectural formula of the arcade over the pillar serves both a structural and an ornamental purpose.

Bottom of the page: a contemporary view of the Colosseum from above.
Opposite page: the Tabularium and other monuments at the foot of the Capitol, from a reconstruction by C. Moyaux in 1866. L'Ecole Nationale Supérieure des Beaux-Arts, Paris.

was tightly joined to those near to it and anchored to the ones below with numerous iron braces and pins, fixed with lead, for which about 300 tons of the metal were required.

In the building of the Colosseum, and in particular in its lower sections, wide use was made of tufa squares, while almost all the elevation and dividing walls were made of brick.

In order to have the amphitheatre built rapidly, the architect applied a revolutionary concept of division of labour on four independent sites, one for each quadrant, and separated the erection of the load bearing structure from the work of filling and plugging. This second expedient allowed subdivision of the work in successive storeys and therefore into autonomous sections operating in union. It is possible to deduce that such a work procedure was adopted, from the independence of the many travertine pillars from the tufa and brick structures and above all from the defective links between the sites, very noticeable in the travertine 'skeleton' where the outside walling has collapsed.

Cement conglomerate was used in an unprecedented quantity: in the supporting vaults of the cavea, for the walls and most of all in the imposing foundations.

The construction required an unprecedented use of wooden scaffolding as well as a large number of lifting machines. Every worker had to complete to perfection his own work in order to have the structure maintain homogeneous stability, growth and solidity. What we have seen leaves us to suppose that the skilled workers who laboured on the erection of the Colosseum must have been very specialized.

Therefore the story according to which 15,000 Hebrew prisoners had been carried forcibly to Rome after the conquest of Jerusalem, to be used on the site of the amphitheatre, can be discounted. Certainly it did not suit the Roman state to send in crowds of servile, heterogeneous and disheartened workers to erect its monumental works. It is possible that this tradition may have sprung from the fact that the Flavian emperors glorified themselves in the conquest of Jerusalem, while Hebrew tradition, seeing in the Colosseum the most representative of the Flavian symbols, imagined it erected with the toil of its exiles.

THE FOUNDATIONS AND THE DRAINAGE

The marshy nature of the valley and the geological inconsistency of the soil caused not a few problems at the beginning of the construction of the great Flavian Amphitheatre. Furnishing the building with a normal foundation would have caused it to subside deeper and deeper into the mud, under its own weight. Investigations conducted in 1978 ascertained that the Colosseum foundations are made up of a continuous bed of concrete with flint chips, interrupted at intervals by small drains, part of the complex system of water downflow from the monument. This foundation finished near the exterior with a mighty brick wall, about three metres thick and six metres deep, into which was set a series of collectors and sewers for the outflow of the water. In the annular portion, which had to bear the weight of the terraces, the concrete bed was covered with a sort of pavement of travertine

blocks, about 90 centimetres thick and laid like a donkey back, to allow for the drainage of storm waters both towards the exterior and the interior. On this travertine floor the spaces for each pillar were traced with incised lines. Then, where it was necessary, the delimited squares were levelled and linked by leaded iron cramps. The lower part of the pillar was successively pinned and welded with a lead casting, whose little adduction channels can still be seen. Several drillings have indicated that the thickness of the concrete bed is about 12.4 metres.

The organization of the sewer network was of great importance in the work of land reclamation and of maintenance of the structures. As far as the elevated part is concerned, the rain water catchment system consisted of a series of concentric elliptical ducts distributed at various levels and linked by wells to the ground floor of the building. The great quantity of water deposited onto the terraces and the arena floor was carried through a series of vertical conduits to the hypogea, from where the main sewer system branched. Within the foundation bed, the cisterns for five big collection drains had been constructed inside wooden casings: one ring-shaped, following the building perimeter, and four radial, which, starting from the centre of the arena, followed the main axes of the ellipse. The dimensions of the four radial ducts are remarkable, about 1.30 × 1.80 m; for this reason it has been assumed that they were planned during the time of Vespasian in order to provide for a rapid outflow of the water which had to flood the hypogea to permit the performance of the naumachias. Later on, Domitian, giving up the idea of performing water-shows in the amphitheatre, had the collectors

A fourth century carved marble slab featuring two gladiators (a secutor *and a* retiarius*) and scenes of* venationes. *The Colosseum Antiquarium.*

paved over with 'bipedal' bricks, (measuring two feet by two feet) had their slope modified and constructed the hoists which were needed for the performance of the *ludi* in the arena. In recent years the excavations relative to the two northern and southern collectors, in the various stratifications sealed by plaques of mud, have resulted in the recovery of very interesting objects testifying to arena life: fruit stones, seeds, pieces of bone, fabrics and wooden fragments. The study of these finds has shown what kind of animals were killed during the shows: there were both domestic animals like chickens, pigs, dogs, oxen and deer, and wild animals, such as lions, bears and panthers. While the biggest animals were used in the course of the games, those of the farmyard were essentially used for cooking by the servants crowding the lower floors of the arena. It is for this reason that some of the bones found show traces of burning; they were in fact animals cooked to be eaten. Besides animal bones the collectors have also given up, as we have said, numerous seeds and fruit stones relative to the food consumed on the slopes by the spectators during the performances. The accumulation of rubbish along the collectors caused the exit to be osbtructed. Drain water began to stagnate and from the fourth century the deposit of everyday waste and mud built up which soon led to the complete obstruction of the conduit. The excavations gave an opportunity for the study of the techniques used in the construction of the collectors. The cistern was built with an oak casing, then incorporated in the foundation concrete, while the covering was inclined by the same technique.

THE EXTERIOR

Around the amphitheatre there was an area paved in travertine 17.60 m. wide, bounded by stones, also of travertine, fixed into the ground and cut into a semicircle on the top. Five of these stones found in 1895 are still there, facing the XXIII, XXIV and XXV arcades looking towards the Celius. On their inside face are the grooves for the winches operating the *velarium*. Beyond this floor began the basalt street brick. The mass of the Colosseum rises over a two-stepped stylobate to a height of four floors; the first three have an ordered series of arches, while the attic has rectangular windows. Each of the first three floors has eighty arches of Tuscan (a Doric version), Ionic and Corinthian order, interposed with semicolumned pillars that project for two thirds of their diameter on the first two floors, but only for half on the third. Between each order runs a cornice surmounted by a slightly protruding attic, which forms the base of the next level. The fourth floor, stressed by Corinthian pilaster strips has one rectangular window in every second compartment, giving a total of forty. The eaves incorporate strong brackets in the frieze and are decorated in architrave style with three fillets and a cyma ending at the top with a grandiose drip stone. The capitals of the three different orders, like the cornices, are roughly wrought, as the distance at which

they would be observed would not permit distinction of detail. The ground floor barrel-vaults are numbered except the four corresponding to the axes, of which the two on the major axis were the main entrances to the arena, while the second two relative to the minor axis were reserved for the imperial seating. Today 42 arches survive from XIII to LIV, of which 38 have collapsed. The numbers helped the spectators to identify quickly which section of the cavea and which staircase was assigned to their social class. It is interesting to note that every four arches there was an inner staircase ending in a *vomitorium*, an exit onto the cavea that showed, carved in the arch, other reference numbers. Number 'I' is on the right, number LXXVI to the left, looking at the monument from the Celius side. In front of the barrel-vault that constitutes the northern entrance on the minor axis, can be seen the remains of two big column bases, which once formed a marble entrance-porch, possibly crowned by a *quadriga* (chariot drawn by four horses) as appears on some coins and reliefs. Probably also the other entrances had the same aspect. Unfortunately there remains an unsolvable question as to whether a statue rose in front of each arch, since in traditional iconography barrel-vaults are enlivened by figures; but in the position on the floor there are no traces of pinning or pedestals. The attic decoration was entrusted to 40 gilded bronze shields, possibly representing god heads, hung on the wall alternating with the rectangular windows. The whole exterior of the building is constructed in travertine square work, with dry blocks, held together by metal pins and cramps.

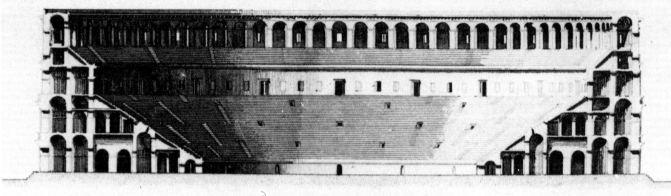

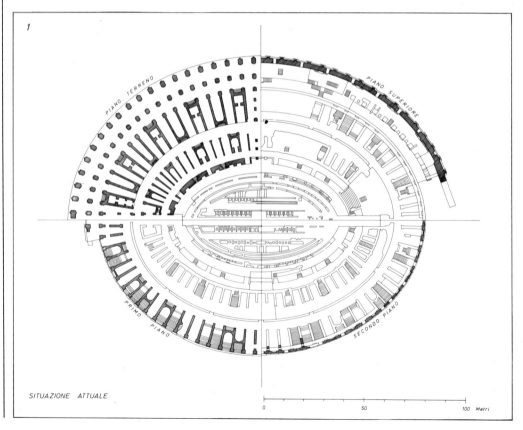

1

PIANO TERRENO

PIANO SUPERIORE

PRIMO PIANO

SECONDO PIANO

SITUAZIONE ATTUALE

0   50   100 Metri

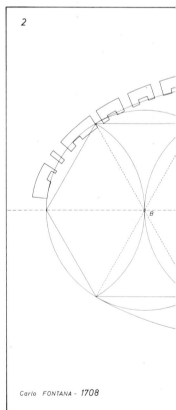

2

Carlo FONTANA - 1708

Opposite page, above: Giuseppe Antonio Guattani's reconstruction of the Colosseum, from a print by Domenico Pronti. Below: 1: a contemporary map of the monument.

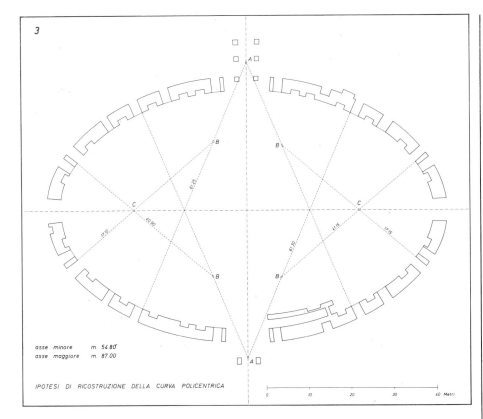

asse minore   m. 54.80
asse maggiore m. 87.00

IPOTESI DI RICOSTRUZIONE DELLA CURVA POLICENTRICA

0   10   20   30   40 Metri

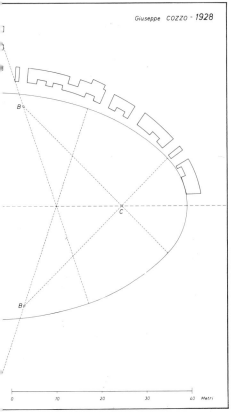

Giuseppe COZZO - 1928

0   10   20   30   40 Metri

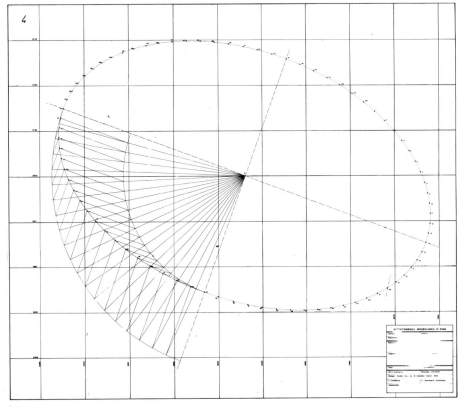

Centre and above: three hypothesis relative to the realization procedures of the ampitheatre curve. 2: the reconstruction made by Giuseppe Cozzo (1928) on the basis of Carlo Fontana's studies and reliefs (1708), compared to the Colosseum's present condition. 3: a hypothetical reconstruction realized by Isabella Diotallevi (1989). 4: a computerised elaboration.

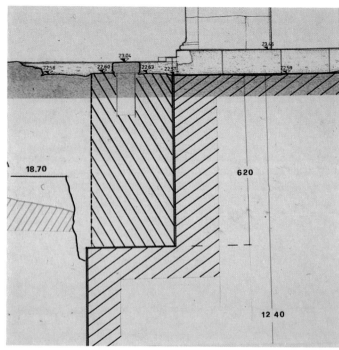

THE INTERIOR

Nowadays it is possible, thanks to the almost complete absence of the cavea steps, to see the bare structure of the building and the areas below the arena, covered originally by wooden boarding, on which wild beasts and gladiators fought to the death.

The south-east entrance was the *Porta Libitinensis*, since on that side the II Celimontana region was developing. This is where the *spoliarium* was, the place to which dead or mortally wounded gladiators were carried in order to be finished off and despoiled of their costumes and arms.

The dead animals were carried out through the same door. These were normally given to the *bestiarii* who shared out the edible meat, skins and bones.

Large animals, such as the elephant, rhinoceros and hippopotamuses which were too big for the hoists, were also brought into the arena through this door.

At the north-west end of the major axis opened the *Porta Triumphalis* through which the *pompa gladiatoria* entered before the games began.

As for the distribution of stairs and corridors on the first two levels, there are two ring-shaped

Top left: a detail of the pillar foundation on the floor's travertine stones. The carved lines mark the exact point of entry of the vertical element.

Top right: graphic relief with a detail of the join between the foundations and the detached pillars. The lines caused by the discharge of the water are also visible.

Above: a detail of the oak moulds used for the construction of the sewer network.

Right: a detail of an eave in travertine stone.
Below: a detail of the annular drain which runs along the building's internal perimeter.

ambulatories, roofed by a barrel-vault, laid on a slightly projecting travertine cornice. The third architectural level, which was Corinthian, possesses the same two corridors but they are lower.

The radial bearing wall sections of the cavea stem from the ambulatories; on the ground floor they alternate with a passage to the *vomitorium*, a two-flight staircase, through which it was possible to ascend to the higher level, and an understair. The coverings of the external ambulatories are barrel-vaulted on the first and third floors, with cross vaults on the second. The aspect of the cavea can only be conjectured, because of the almost complete lack of the staircases and of the divisions between the different sectors. There was a podium all around the arena. It was 3.60 m high, and had square niches on the frontage, as well as a small rainwater-collecting canal. Over it there were two or three rows of marble seats for the most important personalities of the State. The podium was interrupted only by the two doors at the extremities of the major axis. There were boxes at the centre of the curved wings, at the extremities of the minor axis. The south-western one, towards the Palatine, was the *pulvinar*, where the Emperor sat when he was presiding over the games. Exactly in front of this, on the Celius side, was the box of the magistrate delegated by the emperor to substitute for him in his absence. Under the imperial podium there was a sunken walk way, vault-covered and decorated with stuccoes and marble slabs, called 'Commodus'passage', directly connecting the Claudian buildings on the Celius with the podium itself. The long podium on which the senators sat, together with the major representatives of the political and religious worlds, was richly decorated with marble friezes depicting tripods and altars, while the stair mouths were furnished with balusters in the form of running animals. Since these illustrious spectators were rather exposed to the wild beasts, a very strong gilded metal net was stretched between the podium and the arena: on its upper part were a series of elephant tusks turned towards the arena and some special ivory rolls, which hindered any attempt by the beasts to climb up (we know these details from the writings of the poet Calpurnius in his *Egloga VII)*. In any case, in niches set under the podium were posted two archers, whose essential task was to kill any animal that tried to climb over the net. The terraces constituting the *prima cavea* counted 14 *vomitoria* and were reserved for the representatives of the equestrian order. Then followed the *media cavea* provided at the top with 28 windows to illuminate the back corridor, and finally the *summa cavea*. Each one of these three sectors of the cavea was composed of an *iter* of a different number of steps (12 for the *prima*, 19 for the *media* and seven in the *summa*) and closed at the top by a continuous wall named *praecinctio*.

The cavea was crowned by a portico of 80 cipolin and granite columns, surmounted by capitals of composite and Corinthian order. From an epigraph containing the Acts of the Arval priestly college we know that the portico contained an eleven step wooden gradin known as *maenianum summum*.
The women sat in the portico, while all the rest of the cavea was allocated to the male spectators by wealth.
A much debated question is how many spectators the Flavian Amphitheatre was able to contain. The Regionarian Catalogues of the Constantinean age assign *loca LXXXVII milia* to the building, that is 87,000 places, but it has recently been suggested that this figure should be taken as the linear extent of the terraces in feet, thus assigning to each spectator a space of one and half feet, the number of seats diminishes to about 58,000, much nearer to the real architectural possibilities of the monument. In any case not everyone could count on a seat; it is probable that in the portico there would be another 4 or 5,000 standing spectators. After the fourth century, the assignment of seats no longer took place according to category, but according to family. Every family block had its own name engraved on the step belonging to it. Names were erased and substituted when the places were reassigned to new families. As far as the attic is concerned, it is interesting to notice that in the brick curtain have remained traces of the stairs relative to the wooden gradins and that where the brick is missing the interior of the attic appears to have been built with materials removed from other buildings, above all in the parts restored by Heliogabalus and Alexander Severus.

Opposite page: stylised drawings that illustrate the Doric, Ionic and Corinthian types of column. The latter example is trabeated.

On this page: a detail of the southern imperial entrance. This probably featured a second door surmounted by a quadriga. This has been documented in both coins and bas-reliefs.

On this page: the area inside the Colosseum, as it appears from the imperial entrance. On the opposite page, above: the Porta Libitinensis, through which the corpses of slain gladiators and animals were carried.

Below: a detail of the cavea; notice the section of first class seats which have been restored with original fragments.

THE ARENA AND
THE SUBTERRANEAN AREAS

The arena was of an elliptical plan 87.30 × 54.30 m and of an average depth of 6.10 m from the lowest floor paved in 'fish-bone' small bricks to the podium level. It was subdivided into several areas, defined by walls of tufa and brick and distributed into four sectors by the two corridors placed on the major and minor axis of the ellipse. The series of mural structures, in addition to having the function of supporting the boards of the floor, contained the hoists used during the shows. The Colosseum arena was subject to many changes during the centuries of its use and thus today we can see the situation relevant to

Right: an architectural model of a section of the podium reserved for prominent spectators. The area is equipped with a protective net as well as archery holes. Museo della Civiltà Romana, Rome.
Below, left: a fragment of the podium and, right, a detail of the protective net's support pillars.
Bottom: part of the shaft used by the archers, whose job it was to protect the spectators from the wild animals.

the restorations of the fifth and sixth centuries A.D.

The big tufa and brick sections crossing the whole cavity of the arena had, as has been said, also the task of supporting an elevated wooden floor, composed of many movable boards, on which the actual performances took place.

In the central corridor of the hypogea a complex system of inclines allowed the transportation onto the arena of the large pieces of scenery of mythological inspiration and the wings which had already been prepared underground. In fact, on the vertical walls can be found lines of holes obliquely set, which relate to the lodging of cramps supporting a

wooden 'rail' along which the scenery was made to go up and down.

Symmetrically to the central fascia there were triple rows of trap-doors which, given suitable hoists, permitted the unexpected appearance of gladiators and beasts in the arena.

The rectangular trap-doors were delimited by four little travertine boundary stones, on which were placed as many pulleys which were operated by capstans underground. The arena also contained a large number of small drains which were used for collecting rainwater and for preventing it from reaching the underground machinery. If credit is given to the source which states that some naval fights took place in the amphitheatre, then the use of these drains as a means of allowing a quicker downflow of water towards the collectors is better understood.

In the paving of opus spicatum of the hypogean corridors are inserted large travertine blocks, whose sides average one meter in length and which show on the visible face a small rectangular cavity where was housed the bronze device acting as a pivot for the capstans.

In the underground perimeter fascia a series of wide niches, which were erroneously interpreted as lifts, must have housed the cages for the animals waiting to ascend to the arena.

In some rare cases the coarse greyish plaster is preserved, which had to cover all the hypogean masonry more as an insulation against humidity than as a decorative factor.

The wooden arena floor was strewn with yellow sand (or "arena" in Latin) coming from the Mount Mario (some belive this is the origin of the term "arena").

After each combat there was an interval during which special attendants rearranged or levelled the sand. Martial recounts a tragic episode that befell two young subordinates in the Colosseum; while they were levelling the disturbed sand with a rake, they were torn to pieces by a lion which had escaped from the control of the bestiarii.

Under the amphitheatre main entrances there were four hypogean corridors linking the underground services with the outside, particularly with the service buildings placed in the immediate vicinity. Among these underground passages we know of the one running under the Porta Libitinensis , that led to the great Ludus Magnus barracks of the gladiators, and that towards the Velia where the wooden scenery was prepared.

THE "VELARIUM"

Most of big Roman amphitheatres were completely or partially covered by the velarium, above all to protect spectators from the sun in the hot season. The announcements of gladiatorial games show that this accessory was advertised (vela erunt), surely as a result of public request. We also know that these velaria, composed of long fabric stripes, were extremely manoeuvrable, so much so that they could be hoisted or partially removed according to changed climatic conditions.

In the Flavian Amphitheatre structures one can still identify the velarium operating system. All around the building, at a distance of 17.60 m. one from the other, were 160 travertine blocks, of which only five remain, to which were fixed the

capstans which controlled the ropes that then passed into the merli of the cornice. In fact, on the attic of the outside wall are located the travertine brackets corresponding to the square holes in the cornice through which passed the 240 beams that supported the whole velarium installation, 160 belonging to the blocks and 80, additional ones, placed every other one. From these beams went a system of cords and pulleys capable of unwinding the fabric strips, thanks to the professionalism of a detachment (vexillatio) of sailors, chosen from those of the military fleet stationed at Cape Miseno.

The enormous weight of the velarium required an extreme precision in manoeuvring, also in relation to wind strength. In 1776, in the surrounds of the Colosseum, a marble anemoscope was found which is now preserved in the Vatican Museum. It consists of a block shaped as a regular dodecagonal prism, bearing on its faces the cardinal points together with the indications of the winds coming from each of them.

The exact way in which the velarium functioned and how it was put into action is still a matter of debate, yet we possess enough data to advance a few reconstructive hypotheses. It is probable that from each block placed in the small square around the building extended two ropes, which joined the corresponding beam at the top of the cornice.

From there the ropes descended into the inside of the arena and were all tied to a single element, probably a mobile ring of metal or wood. At a given signal the sailors posted outside put into action the capstans fixed to the blocks and the central ring was raised in the middle of the arena up to an estimated

A view of the arena showing the extent
of its vast underground network. This
acted as a service area for the games that
took place overhead. All the minor spaces,
which were used for storing scenery and
equipment, were divided into main corridors.

The area was also equipped with trap doors
and elevators and these enabled both the
gladiators and the animals to appear suddenly
in the arena. The arena surface consisted
of a wooden floor and this was supported by
the massive internal walls.

Above: a subterranean passageway covered by sections of barrel-vaults. The light appears through the trap doors.
Above right: another view of the underground passage. This structure, which was located next to the main corridor, contained the lifts which carried the animals to the arena.

Right: an underground passage. The travertine stone blocks in the floor contained the bronze outlets which were used for the tension ropes; these controlled the lifts.

height of about 50 m from the ground. In order to spread and wrap up the tarpaulins other sailors placed on the attic used a system of double ropes that went from the additional beams and reached the ring, covering the whole cavea and part of the arena.

THE STUCCOES

Of the stuccoes that decorated, on the inside of the Colosseum, the vaults and walls of the entrances and ambulatories nowadays very little remains, above all because of atmospherical agents and of man's lack of care.

What remains at our disposal, limited for the most part to a few insets on the vaults of the minor axis entrances, do not permit the reconstruction of the whole internal decorative complex. Yet some Renaissance drawings, realized when many of the stuccoes were better preserved and more accessible, give us a general idea of the kind of execution and form, even if it is evident that every artist has given a personal interpretation to the remains. Most of the drawings reproduce the decorative complex of the North entrance towards the Oppius, essentially because of the better state of preservation of the stuccoes. Even today these cover part of the vaults, the lunettes and the end walls as far as the arches of the central passage and of the two lateral entrances marked with the numbers XXXVIII and XXXIX. In the general misfortune the vaults came out best. Even if the legibility of the motifs present inside the lacunars has been compromised, it is still possible to distinguish the distribution of the lacunars themselves; of different sizes,

together they formed a whole pattern subject to diverse variations. There are small single squares, bigger squares with sides double those of the first ones, and rectangles whose surface is twice that of the minor squares. Each archivolt seems to have 14 units. In the central passage the vault was decorated with a large central square lacunar, four small squares on the sides, then rectangles and again squares. All lacunars are delimited by an Ionic cornice with leaves and ovules, and are separated one from the other by large decorated ribs connected by five petal rosettes. We know more about inside decoration from Renaissance drawings, aided by the few remains. There are no doubts about the abundance of Dionisiac elements, like allegories of the seasons (recumbent women with cornucopias), putti, garlands, victories, sea monsters and Nereides, all elements constituting the Bacchic court. The same can be said about the figures relative to the lunettes and to the back walls, which feature scenes with drunken satires, Menades and the discovery of Arianna abandoned on Nassus island. If the confraternity of the cult of Dionysus, a god linked with shows, justifies in itself such decorative choice, it must be remembered that Bacchic scenes can be found everywhere in the public and private buildings of the empire. We can therefore emphasize not so much the decorative but the symbolic value of the Colosseum stuccoes.

As far as dates are concerned, it can be said that we are close to the final phase of Pompeian IV style, therefore in the time of the reign of Titus, who clearly had the first floor areas, which were already finished by his predecessor Vespasian, elegantly decorated with stuccoes.

THE MARBLES

Of the marble elements that decorated in large number the interior of the Flavian Amphitheatre, today practically nothing remains *in situ*; this is essentially due to the despoiling carried out by medieval calcars who obtained lime from the burning of marbles and to the reusage in Renaissance building yards. A few remains recovered in the excavations of the subterranean parts or in the ruin of the cavea denote the existence of marble elements above all in relation to the *vomitoria*, the podium, the seats of the senatorial class and the equestrian order, the *maeniana* separating the different cavea sections and, in particular, to the upper portico *in summa cavea*. Of a sculptural rather an architectural nature are the fragments of the figured reliefs of the podium and the statues of external orders, to which must be added the many inscriptions relative to different restorations or to the various celebrations.

As has already been stated, the most conspicuous marble remnants are those relating to the upper portico, of which about 65 capitals (from the original 80 cipolin columns) remain. Until some time ago it was thought that the portico and the attic had been completed only with Domitian, but it has recently been stated that actually the attic appeared to be finished already with Titus, at the time of the inauguration. In any case, most of the remains are not related to the first Flavian phase, but to a reconstruction most likely datable back to the third century A.D., as the re-use of an honorary Trajan inscription in the execution of one of the capitals seems to document.

Left: one of the so-called 'direction rooms' currently assigned to the Colosseum's Antiquarium. In this enormous area, the games' 'director' and his assistants coordinated everything, sending wings and scenery up into the arena and synchronising the entry of both the gladiators and the animals.
Below: the view along one of the main corridors towards the direction room.

At present, some marble capitals relative to the upper portico are visible in the ambulatories surrounding the arena, deposited there after their discovery together with numerous stumps of the cipolin columns.

From a typological point of view, the capitals can be reunited in various groups, each one pertaining to a different restoration intervention. The most numerous are those realized in composite style with smooth leaves; they are attributable to one of the last large scale restorations towards the end of the third century because of their summary execution and numerical predominance. It is interesting to notice how

Below: the pillars, outside the ampitheatre perimeter, used for maintaining the velarium's tension ropes.
Bottom of the page: a detail of the holes to which the pulleys were fixed.
Right: the ampitheatre's perimetric structure, showing the elaborate system designed to control the tension of the velarium which covered the arena.

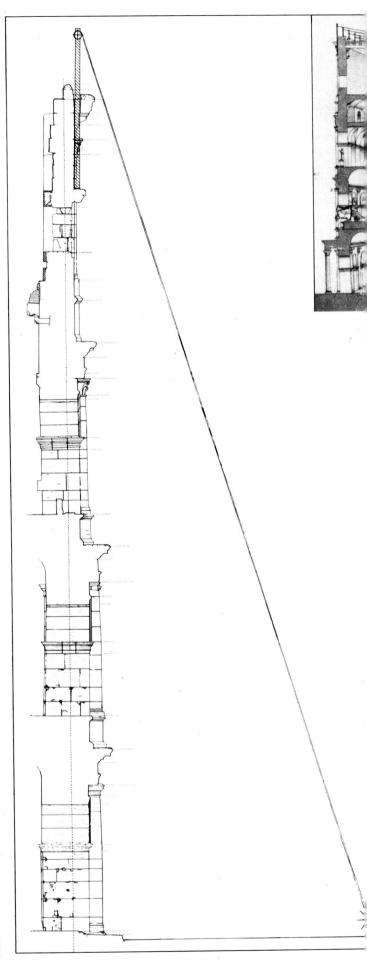

Above: the interior of the Flavian Ampitheatre during a spectacle. The velarium *is drawn in this illustration by Flavio Pio Castellani, c. 1850.*

Above, left and right: details from the attic showing the trabeation, as well as the square holes and the support beams used for moving the velarium's *ropes.*

Left: the base of an anemometer, which was used by sailors and other workers to control the direction of the wind. This helped them in their task of hoisting the various segments which formed the velarium.

35

two examples, almost certainly datable to the beginning of the fifth century, are in the same style. Besides the capitals, inside the Colosseum remain nine Attic basements, almost all referable to the great reconstruction of the portico at the end of the third century. It is also worth noting that not one of the architectural elements found, not even among the most ancient Corinthian capitals, seems to come from the age of the Flavian emperors.

Of less importance are other marble architectural fragments, generally limited to small pieces of architraves, cornices or corbels, belonging to the openings and the niches hollowed out of the dividing walls of the cavea. More monumental and refined in their nature are some fragments of marble baluster preserved in the *Antiquarium* of the monument which emanate from the enclosures of the terraces, near to the access stair outlets (*vomitoria*).

These *transennae*, almost certainly belonging to the first phase, are characterized by spirals of vegetation and by the representation on both sides of hunting scenes or of fantastic animals all the way round.

THE EPIGRAPHS

The Colosseum epigraphic testimonies today reach the conspicuous figure of around 500 pieces, most of which are in a fragmented condition, not easy or impossible to integrate; only in few more fortunate cases we have at our disposal texts either complete or lacking only some parts whose general sense is deducible. They are for the most part inscriptions

engraved on marble slabs, or on blocks belonging to the amphitheatre structure itself. Numerous inscriptions were placed there during the working period of the structure, but modern inscriptions can also be found, such as the tablets affixed in the last century by the popes that had the monument restored. We can distinguish among the ancient inscriptions two categories: functional epigraphs, generally displaying a brief text, whose aim was that of giving directions relative, for instance, to the regular flow of spectators; commemorative epigraphs, pertaining to particular celebrations or to restoration interventions.

Unfortunately most of texts refer to the last working period of the amphitheatre, between the fourth and the fifth century, while we lack inscriptions relating to its inauguration or to the first phase of its life.

Among the 'functional' epigraphs we can cite the numbers set at the top of the outside arches, to distinguish the various entrances, to sort out the influx of the public. This same regulation must have been repeated more accurately inside; this is indicated by a fragment of baluster, in which is engraved the inscription that the place was reserved for the inhabitants of Cadiz. Yet the most interesting inscriptions in this category are surely those quoting the names of the senators, who from the end of the third

century began to have their names engraved on the terrace reserved for them. More important from an archaeological-monumental point of view is the great inscription of Theodosius II (401-450) and Valentinian II (425-455), referring to the extensive restorations carried out by Flavius Sinesius Gennadius Paulus. It concerns the parapet crowning the podium, of which remain nowadays about 130 marble fragments along the northern edge of the arena. Probably the restorations followed the earthquake of 442 or 443 A.D. The text states: "For the attainment of every success by our two sovereigns, Flavius Theodosius and Placidus Valentinianus, eternal most invincible princes, Flavius Sinesius Gennadius Paulus, most eminent and illustrious senator, prefect of the town, for the second time awarded the faculty of delivering judgements in place of the Emperor's sacred majesty, having eliminated the waters through ways not existing before, restored and dedicated the podium and the lower part of the amphitheatre, in order to render greater the satisfaction and pleasure, by reason of the state of beatitude of the present age".

Another epigraph, in the name of the same Emperor, refers to the works executed by prefect Rufus Cecina Felix Lampadius, a relative of the already mentioned Flavius Sinesius, who had carried out, around 444 A.D., an almost total reconstruction of the arena. This inscription, engraved on a big block of marble and found in the corridor under the *Porta Libitinensis,* is today laid on the opposite side, close to the right wall of the western entrance.

Opposite page: part of a marble sarcophagus which was found inside the Colosseum. Like many examples of funereal material, it was to become calcified in the medieval period.

Below: a marble fragment sculpted on the balustrade of one of the entrance corridors. Carvings on the back tell us that these seats were reserved for the inhabitants of Cadiz.

Left: a plaque with an epigraph placed in the Colosseum by Pope Gregory XVI (1765-1846).
Below: an inscription with the number 52 indicating one of the entrances through which the spectators, who had each been assigned a token, passed before taking up their seats.

Left: a seat with an inscription that indicates the places reserved for a few senators.
Below: a fragment of a monumental epigraph commissioned by the emperors Valentinian (425-455 A.D.) and Theodosius (401-450 A.D.). This commemorates various works of restoration which were probably made necessary by the earthquake of 442-443 A.D.

One of the last pieces of epigraphic evidence about the life of the Colosseum dates back to the end of the fifth century, after the fall of the Western Empire. The epigraph, originally preserved in three copies, informs us about the last ancient restorations achieved by urban prefect and ordinary consul Decius Marius Venantius Basilius (consul in 484 A.D. under the king of the Erules, Odoacres) or by his homonymous son (consul in 508 A.D. under the king of the Ostrogoths, Theodoric). This inscription, cut with rough and imprecise characters on two statue bases now placed under the amphitheatre's western entrance, mentions an earthquake and some subsequent restorations:
"Decius Marius Venantius Basilius, most eminent and illustrious senator, urban prefect, patrician, ordinary consul, reconstructed at his own expense the arena and the podium, that the ruin of an abominable earthquake demolished".

THE ICONOGRAPHY

The Colosseum, being one of the most celebrated monuments of Roman antiquity, had a considerable fortune also in the iconography, and was represented on reliefs and on some coin issues. These representations are naturally a very important source for the archaeologists, who can gather much information about the aspect of the monument in various ages.
One of the most notable is that depicted on one of the marble slabs that once lined the sepulchre of the Haterii on the Via Labicana, now in the Vatican Museums and datable to the height of the reign of Emperor Domitian (about 90 A.D.). On this

slab are represented some monuments, that, according to the most common hypothesis, were built by the *redemptor* (building contractor) Quintus Haterius.
The penultimate building from the right can almost certainly be identified with the Flavian Amphitheatre, even if in the representation doesn't entirely correspond to our archeological knowledge, or indeed to the monument itself. The order of the capitals is wrong; it appears as Ionic on the ground and first floors and composite on the third; the ground floor columns are shown standing on a high moulded plinth; on the attic is pictured a low baluster without the order of pilaster-strips, instead of the high side wall with big quadrangular windows; finally the series of eagles under the barrel-vaults of the last floor are anomalous, having never been mentioned by any source. Many aspects would lead us to recognize in the building the Colosseum before the presumed Domitian enlargements, but since we now know that the attic had already been completed in its present forms under Titus, we are inclined to consider the inaccuracy as simplifications or mistakes of the sculptor.
The other useful iconographic source consists of coins, even if great attention must be paid to the degree of reliability of such stamped representations, given the scarcity of available space offered by a coin. It is then possible that certain coins show details rendered in a rather symbolic way, not completely faithful to the original monument.
Coins representing the Flavian Amphitheatre are of four issues, included in the period 80-244 A.D., from the reign of Titus to that of

Gordianus III. The first coin is a bronze sestertius issued by the Senate on the occasion of Titus' eighth consulate (80 A.D.), representing on the obverse the Emperor sitting on the curule saddle, while on the reverse is the amphitheatre seen from outside with a partial view of its interior, to the prejudice of the correct perspective. The representation of the attic is particularly interesting.
Until recently most historians thought it had been the work of Domitian, but here it is already complete with pilaster strips, large windows and even the shields. Outside are the two nearest monuments to the Colosseum: the *Meta Sudans*, the monumental fountain of singular conical shape on a circular base, and a porticoed building of two orders. The next coin, a senatorial sesterce, dates back to the time of Alexander Severus (222-235). Here the amphitheatre has a more summary appearance, deprived of many details and with a strange doubly sloped covering on the attic porch. The last coin figuring the Colosseum was a bronze medallion of Gordianus III Pius (238-244), not real currency and of limited issue. In this case too on the obverse of coin was the Emperor's laureate profile with the amphitheatre on the reverse. Here the outside is drawn summarily, to bring into evidence what is happening inside the arena: a fight between a bull and an elephant carrying a human figure on its back. It would appear that the Emperor is a spectator to this conflict. At the left of the Colosseum is the *Meta Sudans* and, behind it, the huge radiate Colossus; on the left is the porticoed building, here with only one order, interpreted as the entrance to the Thermae of Titus.

More than any of Ancient Rome's monuments, the Colosseum has attracted the attention of artists and architects of every era. On the opposite page: a view from the Oppian hill and, on the left, the interior of the Colosseum as seen by Gaspar van Wittel (1655-1736), one of the principal landscape artists of the eighteenth century. Private collection.

Below: the Colosseum from the Farnese Gardens, one of the many Roman landscapes painted by Jean-Baptiste Corot (1796-1875) during his first Italian sojourn (1825-1828). The Louvre, Paris.

FROM DECLINE TO REVIVAL

The advent of Christianity obviously conditioned the existence of the Roman monuments. In 392 A.D., the Emperors Theodosius I and Valentinian II, in forbidding any form of pagan sacrifice, even the cult of the Lari, effectively condemned the temples, which were subsequently closed and deprived of maintenance.

On the other hand, even if almost all Christians were averse to gladiatorial games, this kind of show continued to take place in the Colosseum arena: it happened either because of the great fascination that the game exerted on the crowds, or because many Romans remained pagans, above all those belonging to the most conservative families.

In 399 A.D. the Colosseum was still efficient, as can be seen from the fact that Flavius Manlius Theodorus, in order to celebrate his consulate, had some hunts arranged there; in the same way it was still functioning in 519 A.D., when Eutaricus, son-in-law of Theodoricus, celebrated his consulate with great feasts and *venationes*.

Later information about the use of the monument, even if indirect, is given in a letter of Cassiodorus, in 523 A.D., sent to consul Valerius Maximus, from which it results that at that time *venationes* were still considered among the principal forms of entertainment, notwithstanding their intrinsically heathen character.

It must therefore be stressed that the amphitheatre remained in function even after the conversion of Rome: such performances were so rooted in popular customs that it would have been inadvisable to abolish them.

But soon, because of the Gothic war (535-553 A.D.), political and economical conditions were created in Rome such that the harmony between the ancient city and the new historical reality could no more be maintained; for this reason only those buildings that could be adapted to the new needs were restored and maintained, while the others were denied any ordinary maintenance whatsoever. In synthesis, therefore, it can be asserted that the Flavian Amphitheatre remained in use until the period of the Gothic wars, but that already from the fourth century the water outflow collectors were obstructed.

This obstruction was such that the paving of the hypogea began to be saturated with stagnant water and slime until the complete blockage of the collectors and the subsequent abandonment of the rooms. We do not know whether the filling of the arena, certainly complete in 1332, when a bull fight was held there on the occasion of Ludovic the Bavarian's arrival in Rome, happened naturally, as a consequence of water stagnation and of collapses of parts of the building, or whether it underwent some regularisation, maybe by the Frangipanes who used it as a fortress from 1084.

As happened to almost all ancient monuments, the record of the Colosseum from the sixth to the eleventh century was lost; in fact no literary source at our disposal mentions it in this period of time. An indirect witness of its disuse is the birth of a Christian graveyard, dating from the first half of the sixth century, just in front of the imperial entrance towards the Esquiline. And yet in the Middle Ages the Colosseum was cited as one of Rome's seven wonders. In the guides and the itineraries for pilgrims, the *Mirabilia urbis Romae* drawn up after the year 1000 the amphitheatre was attributed the function of a round temple with a large gilded bronze cupola. The Colosseum was therefore identified with the *Templum Solis* and its construction

as attributed to Virgil, on whom magic and prophetic powers were also conferred. For a long period it was thought that the monument sheltered demonic power and impure spirits. In the humanistic culture and in the Renaissance, the myth of witches, linked to the fabric, remained alive. Even Benvenuto Cellini paid the price one night when he went to the arena in order to evoke some devils. These, he hoped, would win him back the heart of a beautiful Sicilian girl called Angelica. Unfortunately Cellini took fright when he was unable to banish the demons.

"FRANGEPANIS AMPHITHEATRUM"

Near the end of the eleventh century the Flavian Amphitheatre come back 'to life', though with a function very different from the original. In fact in 1084, during the struggle for the investitures, while Pope Gregory was besieged in Castel St. Angelo by the imperial troops of Henry IV, Robert the Guiscard came to his help, and at the head of his Norman troops succeeded in freeing the pontiff and chasing the emperor from the city. But the Romans rebelled against the Guiscard and after harsh strife also the Norman captain and the pontiff had to quit the city and take refuge in Salerno. On that occasion many Roman monuments, whose characteristics lent themselves to

On the opposite page: the Colosseum and the surrounding area, showing one or two buildings and orchards, in the map of Rome drawn by Stefan du Perac, published by Antoine La Lafrery in 1577.

On this page, above: the ruins of the Colosseum, in an anonymous copper plate print (c. 1820); below: the arch of the inner ring and a view of the arena with youngsters climbing on the ruins in an anonymous aquafortis (c. 1780).

43

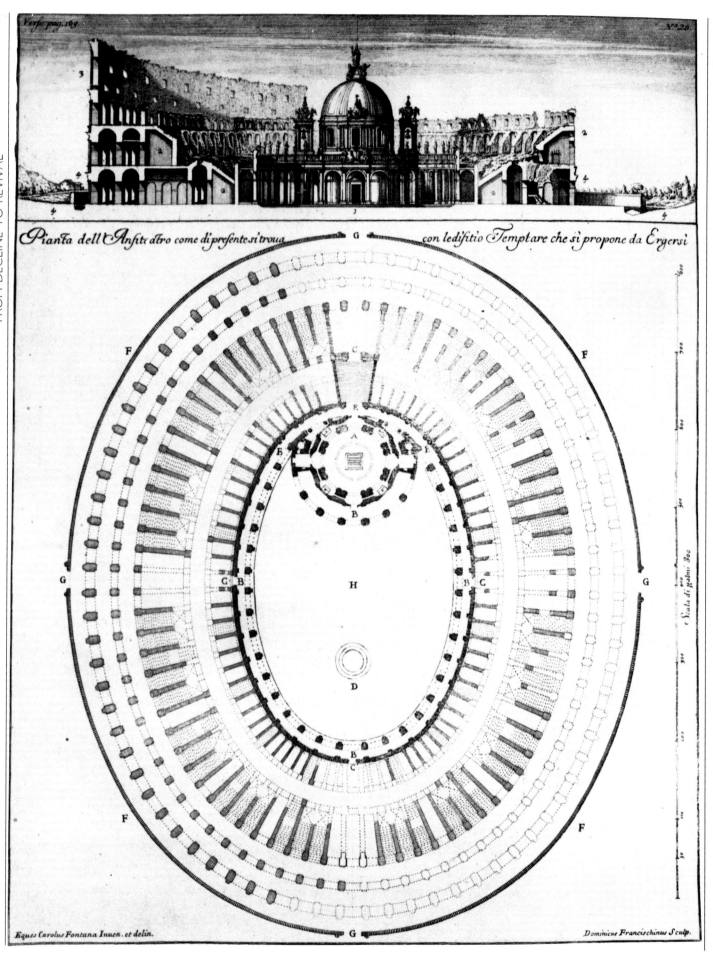

Opposite page: details of Carlo Fontana's (1634-1714) restoration project which the architect realized on commission by Pope Clement XI. The project foresaw the construction inside the eastern section of the arena of a temple to the memory of the Holy Martyrs. The project, which was never realised, was published at The Hague in 1725.

fortification, fell into the hands of noble Roman families who used them as fortresses. Take the case, for instance, of the great Adrian building, which was occupied by the Orsini, of the Augustan Mausoleum and the Constantine Thermes, that became the possession of the Colonnas. The Colosseum was occupied, together with the Septizonium, by the Frangipanes family, who made it the fulcrum of their dominion over the whole surrounding area, fortifying also the Arch of Titus (included in a group of houses of their property, that took in also the Chartularia tower) and that of Constantine. In fact the amphitheatre, which remained in Frangipanes' hands almost uninterruptedly till 1144, situated right on the shoulders of the Lateran, permitted an easy defence either from outside incursions, coming from the Asinara gate, or from possible inside attacks. Moreover, the Frangipanes zone of influence extended over the whole Palatine up to the Circus Maximus, where they owned a mill over the stream crossing the valley.
In 1143, on the death of Innocent II, a popular revolt headed by Arnold of Brescia abolished the temporal power of the popes over the city and re-constituted the Senate. In the tumultuous events that followed, during which two pontiffs, Celestine II and Lucius II perished in the space of two years, the Senate claimed for itself the ownership of the ancient monuments, particularly those fortified: among these was the Colosseum, as a letter of the Roman Senate to Konrad III of Swabia testifies. The Senate incorporated also the college of the *magistri aedificiorum*, whose task it was to take care of the maintenance and restoration of monuments. In 1154, however, Frederick Barbarossa,

invaded Italy at the request of pontiff Adrian IV and suppressed the Roman Senate. Thus the Frangipanes were able to re-take possession of the Colosseum; in 1159 the new pontiff Alexander III was sheltered there in the course of the struggle that they carried on against the antipope Victor IV.
In 1216 the Colosseum was still in Frangipanes' hands: in fact in that year Pietro Annibaldi had a tower built near the amphitheatre in order to be able to assault and conquer it. It should be noted that this tower is still indicated on the Bufalini's map of 1551.
The rivalry between the Annibaldis and the Frangipanes for the possession of the Colosseum lasted many more years, with alternate fortunes. When in 1241 Frederick II tried to conquer Rome, after a siege in which Pope Gregory IX himself died, the Annibaldis managed with the Emperor's support to force the Frangipanes to yield to them half of the Colosseum and of the adjacent palace. Yet on Frederick's death, in 1250, the new Pope Innocent IV, on request from the Frangipanes, declared null and void their contract with the Annibaldis.
Later on the Annibaldis, between the end of the thirteenth century and the beginning of the fourteenth, succeeded in taking possession of the monument again, but were obliged by Henry VII, who came to Rome in 1312, to return it to the Holy See, who in turn put it under the jurisdiction of the Roman Senate. Nevertheless, the Frangipanes retained the properties around the amphitheatre, which they later sold to Orso Orsini.
In 1332, on the occasion of Ludovic the Bavarian's arrival in Rome, the Senate organized in his

honour a bull-hunt in the Flavian Amphitheatre; suitable boxes were prepared and proclamations were issued in Rome and in its outskirts. The crowd was enormous and the Colosseum performed its ancient role for the last time in its history.

THE 1349 EARTHQUAKE

The Colosseum had already suffered considerable damage from the earthquakes which had happened during the pontificates of Deodatus (615-618), Benedictus IX (1047-1048) and Gregorius VII (1073-1085), and was once again violently shaken by that of 1349, which caused some arches of the outside circle to tumble. No such fall is confirmed in our sources, but it can be considered possible on the basis of some sure historical information. In fact, from Bede's famous prophecy *«Quamdiu stat Colysaeum stat et Roma, quando cadet Colysaeum cadet et Roma, quando cadet et Roma, cadet et Mundus»*, it may be deduced that in the eighth century the monument was still intact. It should have been so also in the twelfth and thirteenth centuries, if the Frangipanes and the Annibaldis fought for decades for its possession. A further confirmation comes from a letter of Petrarch, in which, referring precisely to the 1349 earthquake, he said: "Fell that mass which it seemed ought to have seen the world's last day." It is evident that the reference can only be to the outside arches of the amphitheatre, as appears to be confirmed also by two documents of the second half of the fourteenth century. The first one is a letter, dated 1362 from the Bishop of Orvieto Egidius D'Albornoz, papal legate in Rome, to Pope Urban V,

Opposite page, above: an eighteenth century print (from a drawing of the Pannini school) shows the Colosseum during an important period in its history. The arena was consecrated in 1749 to the memory of Christ's Passion and the construction of chapels in honour of the Via Crucis was also commissioned by Benedict XIV at about this time.

Below: a mid-nineteenth century view of the arena, when it was still covered. The aediculae (small shrines) were to remain in place until modern excavation works began on the underground passages.

where the cardinal complains of not having found many buyers for the Colosseum stones he had put up for sale. The second document, more or less contemporary with the first, testifies to the existence of negotiations between the opposing Roman factions for the partition of the travertine that had been 'excavated' from the Colosseum. During the period of the popes' residence in Avignon, the Colosseum and its surroundings had become the abode of criminals, thieves and prostitutes. The task of 'cleaning up' the area was entrusted to the Brotherhood of Sts. Saviour ad Sancta Sanctorum. The pitiless surveillance of these 'guardians' over a long period resulted in the restoration of the district, so much so that the Senate, as a sign of gratitude, decided in 1381 to give the Brotherhood one third of the Colosseum. Still to this day a coat of arms with the image of the Saviour is affixed to the key stone of the entrance arch to the Colosseum on the Lateran side. At this date the property of the amphitheatre was subdivided into three parts: one part to the Roman Senate, one to the Apostolic Chamber and one, as we have said, to the Brotherhood of the Saviour. The concession of one third of the fabric to the Brotherhood was reconfirmed on 28th June 1604 by the Roman Senate, in recognition of that Brotherhood's donation to the Roman people of "the price of the stones used in building the new Capitoline Palace". After the collapses caused by the 1349 earthquake, the parts adjacent to the destroyed arcades began to fall down. Pope Paul II thought it right to utilize the fallen marble in the construction of the Venetian Palace. Moreover, according to the Adinolfi, he also gave "permission to

some of his architects to enable them to demolish several arches of the Colosseum". When Martin V, at the end of the Avignon period, arrived in Rome on 30th September 1420, the city monuments were by then in ruins, which was why the pontiff issued a series of measures aimed at salvaging them, in the course of a rational urban policy. However, the Saviour Brotherhood maintained their ownership of part of the Colosseum, and could go on undisturbed in extracting marble and selling it. The contradictory policy of the Church in respect of ancient monuments continued also under Eugene IV (1431-1447). On the one hand he cared about protecting the Colosseum (first having two walls built separating and linking it with the church of St. Maria Nova, then forbidding the use of the monuments as a marble quarry); on the other hand, he permitted the restoration of the Tribune of St. John in 1439 using travertine coming from the amphitheatre. Under the pontificate of Nicholas V (1447-1455), the remarkable impulse given to monument building again required heavy sacrifices of ancient edifices, in particular of the Colosseum, many marbles of which were sent to the limekiln. The spoliation reached a particularly high level in the period 1461-62, when in the registers of pontifical payments (Pius II, 1458-1464, had just risen to the papal throne) the formula "to draw marble from the Colosseum" became practically a constant. The Colosseum marbles were in fact re-used in building the Holy Staircase, the Square and the Loggia of Blessings in St. Peter's (whose projected source was indeed the Colosseum!), as well as in the restoration of the city walls and the building of St. Mark's church. At the

same time Pius II issued the bull Cum albam nostram urbem on ancient monument conservation; yet this did not prevent the continued plundering of the amphitheatre. It may be sufficient to note from a 1460 document that a certain Master Bartolomeo from Perosa was ordered specifically to make a cart to carry marble from the Colosseum to the Venetian Palace. The plundering continued for the whole of the sixteenth century; in fact between 1480 and 1550 the "fallen travertines" served not only in the building of the Chancellery and Farnese Palaces, but also in the embellishment of many more Roman palaces, amongst them the Senatorial and the Conservatories. Again in the seventeenth century, with the approval of Urban VIII, the travertines of three and a half arches fallen in 1664 were re-used in the Barberini Palace. Summing up the sense of papal politics in the period so far examined, it may be said that despite the great admiration shown in theory by the pontiffs for ancient monuments and particularly for the Colosseum, in practice economic reason always prevailed. The temptation of acquiring marble material for new buildings at infinitely low prices (and ancient marbles were also used to make lime) had always overcome any consideration of the value of the monument; also, until the eighteenth century, no one had ever conceived the possibility of a restoration.

FROM SIXTUS V TO PIUS IX

When in 1585 Sixtus V was elected pontiff, the Colosseum was completely isolated and excluded from the life of the city. For this

Below: a view of the partially waterlogged arena. Excavation work, which was begun at the start of the nineteenth century, had to be suspended in 1866 on account of flooding in the underground section. Although work could continue once the area had been unblocked by Lanciani, the excavation of the arena wasn't completed until 1938.

Opposite page, above: the remains of the wooden covering which was used as a means of raising the level of the underground area and which was rediscovered during the excavations of the last century. Recent research has shown that the amphitheatre's drainage system was shaky from the start; makeshift measures were needed, such as the wooden flooring. Photo: Parker.

reason the pope at first even planned its demolition (that would have taken place for the Septizonium); but, probably because of popular opposition to the plan, or maybe because he realized that the monument could be exploited for his urban programme, he changed his mind and decided to include it in the itinerary of the seven Roman Basilicas. To this end he drew up a project for the construction of three roads which would link the Colosseum to the Lateran, the Capitol and the Quirinale.

Until Robert the Guiscard's fire in 1084, the zone between the Colosseum and the Lateran was densely populated. After that event the centres of life moved to the bend of the Tiber, to the Capitol and into the Leonine town, while the amphitheatre became a strategic outpost. The numerous interventions of the pontiffs in the fifteenth and sixteenth centuries, though re-structuring the centre of the city and realizing arteries like via Giulia, via del Babbuino and via dei Coronari, never succeeded in involving the Colosseum, which remained immersed in

vineyards. Bufalini's map of Rome shows that in 1551 the isolation remained unchanged; on Dosio's 1561 map some settlements begin to appear in the zone towards the Forum. However, on Du Perac-Lafrery's 1577 map, the amphitheatre is still completely surrounded by cultivated fields, as it is on later maps by Greuter (1618), De Paoli (1623), Maggi (1625) and Falda (1676). On the other hand, on Nolli's 1748 map a line of houses appears in the zone towards the Lateran.
The insertion of the Colosseum in the basilican route would have

Below: one of the iron buttresses inserted in the walls during the last century.
Bottom of the page: a detail from the underground section. The holes in the pillars were used for supporting the wooden covering.

transformed the monument into a place of worship but Pope Sixtus V changed his mind and decided to transform the amphitheatre into a veritable working district which would have permitted, on the one hand, the creation of new jobs, thanks to the installation of a spinning mill inside the monument, and, on the other hand, the urbanization of the zone. Towards the end of 1585 the project was entrusted to Domenico Fontana (1543-1607); it foresaw the setting up of industrial workshops on the first floor of the Colosseum, and of shops and workers' dwellings on the higher floors: the plan included the re-construction of the missing parts of the amphitheatre, in addition to the building of a suitable water conduit and the installation of numerous fountains. Domenico Fontana's project was, however, to remain on paper, since Sixtus V died before it was realized. Not even the opening of the road linking the Colosseum with the Lateran and from there to St. Maria Maggiore

49

Below: a detail of the facade which shows the chaotic state of the marble surface. In the nineteenth century there were various attempts at restoration.
Opposite page: the same fragmentation can be seen in this print of c. 1807, showing the construction of supporting spurs by Valadier and

Camporesi which were commissioned by Pius VII. Bottom of the page: this late eighteenth century painting by Jakob-Philipp Hackert shows Goethe's visit to the Colosseum. The painting also shows the monument's poor condition prior to its restoration in the following century. Museo di Goethe, Rome.

brought any important changes to the zone, as can be observed from the 1593 map of Tempesta.
The grandiose plan of Sixtus V had a paralyzing effect on his successors, who were undoubtedly fascinated by the idea of re-building the amphitheatre; but, because of the enormous costs it involved, no one dared resurrect the project. Nor did anyone want to break off the plan for good by stopping the continuous falls of marble through the use of buttresses or spurs. This indecision resulted in a complete absence of maintenance of the monument and in its further degradation. Moreover,

the arcades of the amphitheatre had become once again the haunt of criminals.

Clement X (1670-1676) was the first pontiff to take a new interest in the care of the Colosseum. He let himself be convinced by Father Carlo de' Tommasi that he should commission G.L. Bernini to execute a project which included, while fully respecting the monument, the completion of a little temple in the centre of the arena in honour of the Martyrs (taking the place of the ancient votive altar dedicated to Jupiter). This intervention (that today we would call conservative, because it avoided disturbing the ancient fabric) was not accomplished, probably for lack of funds and because of the death of the promoter Father Tommasi. Clement X limited himself to closing the Colosseum entrances with wooden gates, to walling up the inside arches of the lower order and to erecting a big wooden cross in the middle of the arena.

In 1700 Pope Clement XI (1700-1721) closed the amphitheatre arcades, using them as a depository of dung required for saltpetre production by a nearby powder factory. The analogy with the 'industrialization' plan of Sixtus V is evident, although at a far more modest level. In 1703, following the earthquake of 2nd February, three arches of the second ring facing the Celius tumbled down and Clement XI profited at once from the 'favourable' occasion by re-using them in the construction of the port of Ripetta. During the pontificate of Clement XI Carlo Fontana (1634-1714) worked out an interesting plan for the Colosseum, which included the building of a temple dedicated to the Holy Martyrs on the arena level on the eastern side. The project, subsequently published at The Hague in 1725, after its author's death, was never

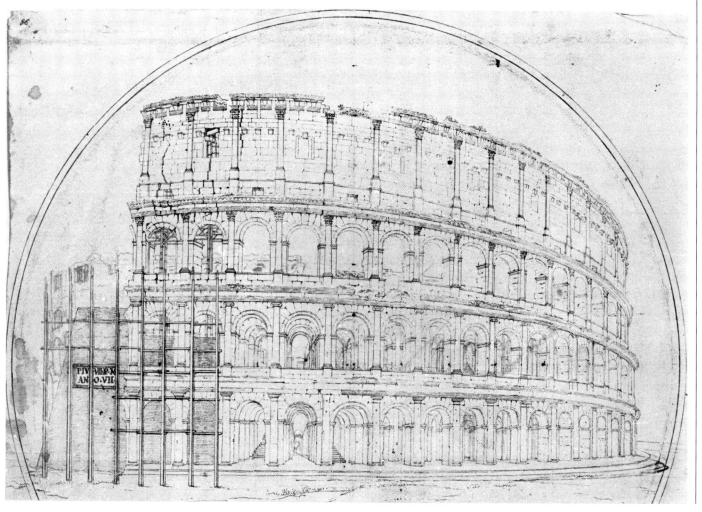

carried out. Among the illustrative plates in the publication the fifth one is particularly interesting; it represents the state of the Colosseum interior in that period. The second volume of Fontana's work is dedicated to the re-creation of the original state of the amphitheatre, with particular attention to information about the functions of the fabric structures.

In 1714 Clement XI repaired the walls, closing the outside arches and the gates of the secondary entrances, that were by then ruined and were again allowing access to malefactors; besides that he also installed two solid wooden doors at the main entrances and provided also for the restoration of the walls closing off the inside arches.

In 1743 Benedict XIV had some restoration work done on the higher floor and around the little church of St. Maria della Pietà sited inside the arena, and arranged to have the walls closing the arches repaired once again.

With the approach of the Holy Year of 1750, there was a remarkable fervour for plans, including that of founding a lay Congregation to erect inside the Colosseum an imposing temple and the chapels of the Way of the Cross and to restore the crumbling sections of the porches and the staircases. Not all of these projects were accomplished, but in 1744 Benedict XIV had an edict issued by the Roman Governor, Monsignor Simonetti, in which the profanation of the Colosseum was forbidden. In 1749, following the persistent requests of Father Leonardo from Porto Maurizio, he consacrated the amphitheatre arena to the memory of Christ's Passion and of his Martyrs and placed the chapels of the Way of the Cross there.

Yet the pontiff, having provided for

the arrangement of the arena, did not effect any consolidation of the vertical structures, so that the urgent necessity of some kind of work to prevent the total ruin of the amphitheatre began to make itself felt. Numerous restoration projects were born, among them that of De Romanis which entailed the construction of a spur at the extremities of the partly ruined outside ring.

However, nothing was done until the part of the enclosure wall facing the Lateran appeared to be in imminent danger of collapse. Pius VII decided to shore it up with a colossal spur. This intervention had the merit of breaking the Church's tradition of immobility regarding the ancient monuments by initiating the application of restoration science to archaeology.

From then on, as we shall see, the consolidation works continued uninterrupted during the reigns of Leo XII, Gregory XVI and Pius IX.

THE POPES AND THE SPURS

Benedict XIV, in declaring the Colosseum a public church in 1749, caused the removal of travertines from the monument to cease. Yet this did not change the fact that it was by then a ruin; in particular the whole outside fascia towards the Lateran threatened sudden collapse because of a total lack of maintenance. Furthermore, from an urban point of view, the amphitheatre was still completely isolated and immersed in wide green spaces, cultivated as vineyards.

These vineyards, that were almost all the property of religious corporations (Novitiate of the Company of Jesus, Carthusian

Fathers etc.), were destined by the regulating plan of 1871 to become a residential zone; a first division into lots was to be in the area between the Colosseum and St. Stefano Rotondo. The subsequent 1873 plan (A. Viviani's work) foresaw, besides massive clearances for the construction of Via dei Fori Imperiali, the birth of a residential quarter between Via Labicana and Via Claudia and of another on the Oppian hill. The 1883 plan extended allocation of lots to the Esquiline and to the Celius where was planned (and accomplished) the building of the Military Hospital; further demolitions were established by the 1909 plan.

The 1923 'general variant' formed the basis for the construction of Via dei Fori Imperiali, which was completed in 1930 by Corrado Ricci. The *Meta Sudans* was razed to the ground by Muñoz and the Colosseum became progressively a traffic-island until the closure of the area between the amphitheatre and the Forum in 1981.

Yet the Colosseum would have certainly fallen into ruin, had not the restorations of the nineteenth century intervened; these progressively consolidated and reintegrated it in some parts by means of reconstructions in brickwork with large iron ties inserted throughout.

The merit of these restorations does not of course go only to the pontiffs of that time who simply interpreted the new ideas of the nineteenth century, the century of archaeology. In fact from its beginning the restorations were started everywhere aiming to stop the decay of ancient monuments. The Colosseum too was involved in this zeal for works, and in 1804 Cardinal Giuseppe Doria Pamphilj discontinued the deposit of dung in

the ground floor ambulatories, thus bringing to an end after so many years the extremely damaging action of saltpetre on the wall structure. This trend towards restoration continued under the French, who effectively governed Rome from 1809 to 1815. In order to solve the old problem of the urban layout of Rome, Camille de Tournon, prefect of the French Government, presented to the Napoleonic administration a vast project that, had it been carried out, would have become the first town plan for modern Rome. As far as the ancient monuments were concerned, he proposed the creation of two enormous archaeological parks, one South of the city including the Forum, Palatine and Murcia valley zones, the other extending from the Pincius to the adjacent districts. A large-scale programme of excavation and restoration was planned for the two parks and this project was entrusted to the respective superintendents.

The Colosseum, according to this plan, restored and surrounded by a square with trees, would have been a part of the southern park, in which the monuments, conforming to an illuministic demand for harmony between nature and history, would have constituted a topographical unity linked by public gardens. The Commission for Public Monuments and Civil Works, meeting on 8th September 1810, prepared a plan of intervention giving precedence to the Colosseum and the Forum and committed the project to the architects Valadier and Camporesi, academicians of St. Luca. The first work to be accomplished was the elimination of the houses and granaries that had risen among the Forum monuments; then came the restoration of the amphitheatre, which closed with its

Top: an aquafortis showing the wooden scaffolding designed by Giuseppe Valadier in 1822 in order to build the outside wall's second spur. The project was commissioned by Pope Leo XII.

Above: a water-colour painted by L. Rossini in 1836 which shows the Colosseum after the completion of the spur. In his restoration work Valadier respected the structure of the monument's arches.

bulk the valley of the monuments. Excavations were carried out to clear the earth which surrounded it and which covered the inner staircases; thus it was possible to make precise reliefs of the monument, like those by Carlo Lucangeli in order to construct the 1:60 scale wooden model now preserved in the Colosseum *Antiquarium.* New supporting walls were built and others that closed off the arches were demolished. When Pius VII was able to retake possession of the Pontifical State after the fall of Napoleon in 1814, he realized that it was necessary to continue the work begun by De Tournon. For this reason he set up a commission whose specific aim was to improve the city's physical appearance. The commission was presided over by Monsignor Rivarola and its members included Fea, Valadier, Camporesi, Stern and Palazzi. The first act of the commission was that of discrediting a project which foresaw the demolition of the unsafe parts. It then presented a paper, which proposed the contruction of a spur at the end of the circle opposite the Celius. This solution responded to the need for solidity and economy.

Pius VII approved the project, even though it presented many difficulties; it was, according to Stern, "the only modern one comparable with ancient brick works".

The construction of the spur was completed in the year 1820. Actually, given the architectural structure of the Colosseum, composed of great rings of superimposed arches supporting one another in opposition (which is why a breach in one of them leads inevitably to the fall of the whole ring), the provision of a buttress to prevent the slipping of already disjointed and tottering travertine, bricks and tufa definitely contributed to the salvation of the monument's outside circle. In order to make monument more visible, it was decided to demolish some of the ramshackle building in front of it. These mainly consisted of hay-lofts. This policy of demolishing the surrounding buildings was to continue throughout the nineteenth century.

the arches in diminishing number upwards from the base in pyramidal fashion. For the execution of this work he prepared a special wooden scaffolding to shore up the unsafe blocks. In order not to disturb the monument's aesthetic aspect, the spur was created in brickwork, but was then coated in travertine (later on this coating was removed). Only some parts, for static and constructive reasons, were executed in real travertine throughout: the whole of the low area of ground floor pillars, the imposts of the arches, the bases of the columns and the capitals.

The outside ring of the south-west sector, looking on to the Celius, had long since collapsed; in this part also the innermost ring (the part adjacent to Pius VII spur) exhibited a great gash through its whole height. Its restoration was supported by Gregory XVI. The project was entrusted to Salvi, who planned to rebuild the seven arches of the first order and the eight of the second order, but based on studies made in other parts of the fabric or, what is worse, on theoretical ideas in the French style. In 1849 Salvi died and the works were continued by a commission composed of Canina, Poletti and Folchi. The restoration was accomplished in brickwork, except for the bases of the pillars and some architectonic details, that were finished in travertine.

After the breaching of Porta Pia, on september 20th, 1870, the authority over Rome's monuments passed to the Royal Superintendence of Antiquarian Excavations, whose director, Pietro Rosa, removed from the structure of the Colosseum "the picturesque mantle of greenery", which covered it with four hundred different plants.

In some respects, the Flavian Amphitheatre was one of the first examples of slum clearance.
In 1822, the successor of Pius VII, Pope Leo XII, decided to build another spur at the end of the outside circle looking towards the *Meta Sudans*.

This section had also collapsed. The work was entrusted to Valadier, who, remembering the great success of his previous 'archaeological' restorations (first of all that of Titus' arch), decided also in this case to respect the building by continuing

THE CIRCUS GAMES

The Romans were very good at absorbing other peoples' customs. When they began their conquest of Italy, their first great adversaries were the Etruscans, an already developed people, who united a passionate interest in the pleasures of life with a constant obsession with death.

Moreover, the Etruscans were extremely superstitious and, to propitiate subterranean divinities, were in the habit of sacrificing prisoners of war to the spirits of the dead. Sometimes they forced designated victims to fight each other to the death.

From the Etruscans the Romans learnt the art of analysing the entrails of sacrified animals and of interpreting the flight of birds. From them they acquired the *fasces*, bundles of twigs tied together with an axe, which were carried in procession by the lictors; from them they took also the golden crown, the purple mantle and the ivory curule saddle, as typical symbols of power.

Again from that mysterious people the Romans got to know the duel-sacrifice, associated with solemn funeral rites. The spectacle, once it was transferred to Rome, progressively lost its religious significance which was substituted by something different and seemingly frivolous: the amusement of a numerous and idle urban proletariat who sought amusement in addition to food and lodging.

At the twilight of the Republic, Roman politicians vied with one another in offering the best gladiatorial shows to the people. The religious tradition was still in certain ways concealed in the games, that were called *ludi* and *munera* (presents).

Even in the imperial age, the attendant charged with ascertaining death, or in some cases with the giving of it by stabbing the defeated fighter with a spear or by striking his forehead with a hammer, took the features of Charon, the ferryman of souls, a Greek, Etruscan and Roman mythological character; or that of Hermes Psychopompus, a Hellenic divinity, who led the spirits of the dead into the underworld.

To render sacred this violent show there were the Vestals, the Pontifex Maximus and the Emperor-God himself, who not only attended the gladiatorial duels, but also

participated, heartily acclaiming his favourites.

The show opened with a chariot parade. Each chariot carried a gladiator wearing a purple mantle embroidered in gold. After they had descended, the gladiators formed a procession marching around the arena. Having arrived in front of the imperial box they shouted: *Ave, imperator, morituri te salutant!* (Hail, Emperor, those who are about to die, salute you!) raising their right arm. Behind the gladiators came the slaves with the combatants' arms and helms. There were several gladiatorial categories, but the most common were the *samnites*, heavily armed in the same fashion as were the terrifying Samnite warriors defeated by Rome in the early days of the Republic. They carrieds swords or spears and *scutum*, similar to the large quadrangular shields of the legionaries. They fought bare-chested, but wore an armlet covering their right arm and a jamb over their left leg, besides the helmet on their head. Then there were the *thraces*, protected by the *parma*, a square or round shield, who attacked with the *sica*, a short curved sword. Another kind of gladiator was the *retiarius*, lightly armed with head, chest and legs uncovered, wearing only a large leather belt on the lower part of his trunk and another on his left arm. His particular arms were a net, in which he entrapped his adversary, and a trident, which he used in order to finish him off. Then there was the

which they put the prize money and that offered by the crowd. The remains of the dead gladiators were much in demand. Their blood was considered a specific remedy against sterility and impotence; the bride whose hair had been unbound with the spear of a defeated gladiator would enjoy a prosperous matrimonial life; an article of the fighter's clothing was useful against the evil eye.

Before Christianity became the religion of the Empire in 330 A.D., the *ludi* were not much criticized. On the contrary, most people felt that the games embodied the ancient Roman virtues of courage, discipline and resistance.

The show was so much loved by the Roman people that many of them, though free men, wanted to feel the intoxication of the arena. Even women were trained for this. Tacitus narrates that in 63 A.D. the gladiatorial *ludi* were splendid as usual "but they exceeded any previous games in respect of the number of illustrious matrons and senators who shamed themselves in the arena".

The authorities had always supported the games, and a whole series of sovereigns had to solve the problem of securing the constant supply not only of men but also of wild animals. The other great passion of the arena spectators was in fact animal-hunts, in particular of wild beasts. The *bestiarii*, the hunters, fought against tigers, lions

---

mirmillo, a name derived from a kind of fish represented on the helmet crest.

There were other categories in addition to these: horsemen, archers, boxers, *bestiarii* for the hunts and others who fought from chariots. The long day in the amphitheatre started with a series of bloodless duels, sometimes bizarre or comic. Arms were almost always wooden and cripples, dwarfs and women fought each other. Then the notes of a *tuba*, the war-trumpet, or of other instruments, announced the beginning of the most awaited performance: that of the gladiators. Real arms had been carefully sharpened; the athletes entered the arena, escorted by managers who had also the task of lashing them with hide whips or red-hot iron bars

if they seemed too hesitant. In the meanwhile, the crowd became uproarious. The ceremonies following victory or defeat were specific: the fallen athlete, for example, begged for mercy by throwing away his shield and raising his left hand. The crowd expressed its verdict which the Emperor confirmed or denied. Once the show was over a table of results was prepared.

The letter P after the name indicated that the gladiator was dead; the letter M, which stood for *missus* ("sent"), signified that he had neither won nor lost but had left the arena on his own feet; the letter V, finally, confirmed that he had won. Winners were given presents, crowns and palm branches, as well as a silver plate in and bears. On a graffito found and preserved in the Flavian Amphitheatre are represented two half-naked men armed with spears who are attacking six savage bears. Far worse was the slaughter of harmless animals such as giraffes, deer and ostriches. When at last the *venationes* were abolished in the sixth century, many animal species had by then disappeared from the regions of the empire: in the Nubia there were no more hippopotamuses; the Ircania had lost its Caspium tigers; from northern Africa elephants had disappeared; in Mesopotamia the mighty lions once represented in Assyrian reliefs had been massacred.

These bloody shows had as their main purpose that of keeping proletarian minds busy. It was an enormous task. Under the Antoninis over one million people lived in

Right: a third century votive lamp in the form of a gladiator's helmet. Museo Nazionale di Villa Giulia, Rome.

Rome, 150,000 of whom were unemployed; also the others lived through long idle periods. In fact, under Claudius there were 150 regular feasts, of which 93 were reserved for the games: moreover, there were triumphs, religious solemnities and imperial parades. For this reason Rome abounded in edifices reserved for amusements: thermae, theatres, amphitheatres, porches, naumachias and circuses. There was the Flaminian Circus, the Gaius Circus, and the Agonistic Circus, but above all that Circus Maximus which Julius Caesar re-built to contain 150,000 people. This latter was enlarged in the first day of the Empire in order to house 250-300,000 people.

The Circus Maximus rivalled the Colosseum in splendour and magnificence. The track covered with golden sand awaited the chariots driven by charioteers dressed in the colours of the respective factions: red, white, blue, green. On the signal of the magistrate presiding over the games, who was distinguished by an ivory stick, a golden garland and a purple toga, the charioteers hurled forward their two, three or four-horses chariots in a desperate run. The names of many famous charioteers, who won more than 2,000 races, have come down to us: Diocles, Epaphroditus Ponticus, Scorpus, Pompeus Muscolosus. Also the most renowned horses were admired and even represented in graffiti and mosaics, always with their manes plaited with pearls. Rome also possessed three great theatres: those of Balbus, Pompeius and Marcellus. Yet in the first and second centuries the crowds ran enthusiastically only to the arenas, the Circus Maximus and the Flavian Amphitheatre. For this reason too, in 222 A.D., in the reign of Alexander

Severus, the Theatre of Marcellus closed its doors. From then on the Roman proletariat sought stronger emotions exclusively in the arena.

THE DEVELOPMENT OF THE "MUNUS"

The programme was usually announced a few days before the gladiatorial games. The *editor* had the *munus* programme painted on the walls of public buildings and houses in the busiest streets of the city, and also on the most visible tombs along the consular roads outside the *pomoerium*. If the organization thought it opportune, and above all on the occasion of particularly spectacular performances, the edict was also written on parchment leaves produced by copyist in great number. These were then distributed in all the city squares, streets and even houses. The physical authors of the *edicta munerum* were persons specialized in painting announcements (the *scriptores*) both of gladiatorial shows and of electoral propaganda. These inscriptions were often real calligraphic masterpieces, revealing great artistic skill. Unlike graffiti, which are a popular and

spontaneous expression of unknown passers-by, the *edicta munerum* were the work of artist-craftsmen who adopted a classical, official form of writing subject to fixed rules. Among the rules was the use of colour, generally red, which was more durable and had more immediate impact on the public. The layout of the text generally respected standard criteria: the name of the *editor*, the *causa muneris* and the beginning of the programme written in bigger characters, these being considered the principal advertising elements. Then the text was traced with smaller but very clear letters up to the final notes and sometimes to the signatures or initials of the *scriptores* or to their joking acclamations written in minute characters or in italics.

The *scriptores* often inserted their own signatures in one of the first letters, the largest that made up the *edictum* (like the 'O' or the 'C'). Various indications were given in the programme. First of all the reason for the games: if they were offered by the Emperor or by a magistrate and also if they were dedicated to a building or a temple inauguration (*ob dedicationem arae*) or to the health of the Emperor (*pro salute Domus Augustae*).

Secondly, the name of the organizer (*editor*); then the number of couples of gladiators, the name of the town where the fighting would take place, the date and some additional information such as the announcement of those entertainments included in the entrance price, among which were the *venatio* and the participation of acrobats.

Lastly, it advised that the *velarium* would be hoisted to prevent the rays of the sun from disturbing the spectators, that the games would be staged only "if weather permitted" and that they would be cancelled in the event of rain or bad weather. The *edictum* ended with a publicity slogan: "This show will be so beautiful that the whole world will want to watch it". Yet, except in rare cases, the names of the gladiators and of the *venatores* entering the arena did not appear in the edict. Generally, the expressions *paria gladiatorum* and *venatio* were considered sufficient to announce the gladiatorial fights. The richness of the *munus* was assessed almost entirely by the number of couples which were presented.

On the eve of the games the gladiators were offered a special dinner (*coena libera*), which the public could also attend. During this dinner the gladiators could indulge every instinct, well aware of the fact that for many of them it could be their last evening. At the end of the banquet they would commit their family to the care of their friends, and arrange for the liberation of their most faithful servants.

On the day of the games, which began in the morning, the gladiators marched (the so called *pompa*) to the roll of drums and the sound of trumpets into an amphitheatre already full of noisy spectators. The *editor* of the games headed the procession with lictors and

LICENTIOSVS

PVRPVREVS·ENTINVS

The gladiators were divided into categories according to their costumes and their weaponry. Here we see scenes of gladiatorial combat in a mosaic from the third or fourth century. The mosaic is from a villa near Tuscolo. Once again the names of the individual athletes are indicated. Galleria Borghese, Rome.

musicians, followed by a *ferculum* or sedan-chair, by the assistants with the prizes for winning gladiators, by servants carrying the most decorated and precious arms and by the stiff gladiators, flaunting their plumes and their glittering costumes. The real fighting was almost always preceded by a fencing exhibition (*prolusio*) with harmless exercise arms (*arma lusoria*). At this moment, private citizens too could go down into the arena to give a taste of their capability. The champions themselves appeared to loosen their muscles and to try some blows. Needless to say, the spectators recognized their favourites and acclaimed them with ovations, while the atmosphere on the terraces and in the arena became inflamed. Before starting the games, the *editor*, in front of the public, made sure that the arms to be used were all strictly according to the regulations (*probatio armorum*). It is known that rules differed according to the period and the ruler. Caesar equipped his gladiators with silver arms; Juvenal tells of the gold bordered tunic of the *retiarius;* the Emperor Pertinax sold off the golden gem-studded arms of his gladiators.

After the controls, the fights began to the sound of such instruments

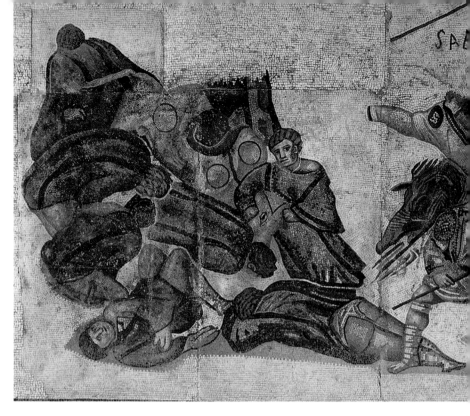

as the flute (*tibia*), the straight trumpet (*tuba*), the curved trumpet (*lituus*), the horn (*cornu*) and even the hydraulic organ (*hydraulus*). Having received the signal, the fighters greeted the Emperor or the *editor*, formed couples, put themselves on guard and, maybe not even looking into each other's eyes, started duelling, carefully observed by referees (*doctores*) and by a screaming public shouting *Verbera!* (hit him!), *Jugula!* (cut his throat!), *Ure!* (burn him!), and, as soon as the blood started to flow, *Habet, hoc habet!* (he has caught him, he has caught him!).

The duel could finish in a variety of ways. When one of the two adversaries died in the arena, two assistants, disguised as Hermes Psychopompus and as Charon, came to take away the corpse.

First they pierced the gladiator's body with a spear to make sure he was dead or, in any case, to despatch him if he was still alive; then with a hook and rope, they tied him to a horse which dragged the body out in the dust. In the more refined shows, the body was placed in a simple coffin and was carried away, through a door used only for this purpose, possessed by all the amphitheatres and called *Porta Libitinensis*, from the arena to the *spoliarium*, a place where it was divested of arms and costumes which were returned to the gladiator's *familia*, or else to his heirs. If the body was not requested by relatives or by the gladiatorial college or by some admirer, then it was buried in unconsecrated ground without funeral honours.

Of course a fight could finish in a different way. It could happen that one of the two gladiators, clearly inferior, dropped his arms, lay down on the ground and, raising his left

hand, begged for mercy. It was a declaration of defeat and from that moment on he was untouchable; his right to live belonged to the *editor*, who, however, in practice handed it over to the spectators. If they shouted *Mitte!* holding up the forefinger (and not the thumbs as normally thought) and waving a piece of fabric or a handkerchief, then they conceded mercy. This had nevertheless to be confirmed by the emperor or by the *editor*. On the other hand, if they shouted *Jugula!*, pointing downwards with the thumbs, the unfortunate man had no alternative but to offer his throat to his adversary for the fatal stroke. This kind of duel, to the death, *sine missione*, was not the only one. It could happen that the *editor*, to preserve his champions, tried to save their lives by not inserting this formula in the programme. Emperor Augustus himself tried to have the practice stopped: he considered it barbarous. But his will was ineffective against the wish for death that excited the crowd.

During the fight it could also occur that the result of the encounter was undecided, that neither of the fighters, being of equal strength or equally wounded, could succeed in prevailing over the other. In this case the crowd would ask for both lives (*stantes missi*) and the two

would leave the arena sadly without honours or applause.

Normally, a victorious gladiator enjoyed a deserved rest, but occasionally he was obliged to fight more than once in one day. This unhappy experience was confined to criminals condemned to death or to men gifted with exceptional strength. Usually the combats were between two gladiators, but sometimes, for a more spectacular choreography, two or more groups were made to fight simultaneously. Caligula had five *secutores* fight against five *retiarii*; Caesar offered games which featured 500 fighters on foot, 300 on horseback and 20 elephants bearing on their backs in turrets men armed with bows, arrows and spears; Claudius ordered the representation of the siege and capture of a town in Britannia. Besides the *Porta Libitinensis*, which as we have seen was the one used for carrying out the dead, every amphitheatre had another gate, the *Sanavivaria*, through which departed those whose lives had been spared and yet another, the *Triumphalis*, for the victors.

The victor, as a sign of rejoicing, raised high his sword; he received as a prize a palm, with which he made a tour of the arena, waving and giving thanks. The more battles he won, the more palm branches he

Another great passion of the ampitheatre spectators was the venationes or hunting. Left: a mosaic showing scenes of combat between gladiators and animals. The mosaic, which is from the third or fourth century, is from a Roman villa near Tuscolo. The name refers to the principal gladiator.

carried in his hands. The public on the terraces threw him coins that he collected and then exhibited on silver trays. The winner also received coins offered by the *editor* and sometimes precious arms. Victorious gladiators gained riches and fame. The patricians considered it an honour to have them as guests; the high-society ladies courted them without restraint. On a Pompei wall it is written that all women in the town passionately longed for a gladiator of the Thracian speciality. The title of infamy linked to their category must have seemed absurd to these gladiators, some of whose names we know (Philargurus, Triumphus). Some of them were even called to serve in the imperial guard. Of course fortune smiled only on a few of the gladiators. Most of them, when age compelled them to stop 'working', were constrained to ask for shelter in the service of the priests of the divinities worshipped by the gladiators. If they did not succeed in this, there remained only begging, maybe under the amphitheatre barrel-vaults. Gladiatorial combats finished either because of lack of light, that is at sunset, or because of lack of 'actors': night performances with the help of illumination seldom took place. It might happen that before

sunset the couples of gladiators taking part in the programme, called *ordinarii*, had finished fighting. In this case the show closed before time among the insults and whistles of the spectators. However, a far-sighted games *editor* would bring into the amphitheatre some substitute gladiators, named *postulaticii*, who had to fight until evening.

THE GAMES CELEBRATED IN THE COLOSSEUM

"The cranes fought one against the other and four elephants and nine thousand wild beasts and sheep were killed, not only by men, but also by common women. Many men fought disguised as gladiators; many groups executed land and naval battles. In the case of the latter, they filled the amphitheatre with water and introduced into it horses, bulls and other docile animals, that were trained to do what they were used to doing on land. Titus also introduced men in ships, who were divided into Corcireans and Corinthians, and who fought in naval uniforms. Others again, outside the city, fought in the wood of Caius and Lucius, that Augustus for that reason had ordered to be prepared. There on the first day a gladiator

fight was staged, and the killing of many wild beasts, on a platform covering part of the lake on the side looking towards the statues; on the outside it was equally surrounded by boarded floors.

The circus games were held the following day: on the third day three thousand men staged a naval battle, which was followed by an infantry combat. The Athenians had overcome the Syracusans (they had fought under these names) and had landed on the island; having assaulted a certain wall that was built around the monument of that place, they took it. These spectacles, so pleasing to the eye, lasted one hundred days. They were also useful to the plebeians, because Titus threw into the theatre from a high place little globes of wood, each of which contained a card referring to food, clothing, a vase of silver or of gold, horses, beasts of burden, domestic animals or servants. Whoever caught one of these little globes, brought it to the dispenser of gifts, and that which was written inside, he obtained".

In this way Cassius Dionis describes the sumptuous feasts offered by Titus on the occasion of the inauguration of the Flavian Amphitheatre in 80 A.D. Suetonius also, describing the life of Titus, tells of the event, confirming that besides the gladiatorial games and the *venationes* the naval battles took place: *in veteri naumachia*.

The sea battles and the number of animals killed did not seem improbable to Giovan Battista Nolli, who, reasoning in strictly mathematical terms, expressed himself as follows: "The two diameters of the arena were respectively 450 and 305 architectonic palms. The whole arena area was 107,795 square palms. On the supposition that the

Below: the circus games in a fourth century
Roman bas-relief from Obzor, Burgas.
The Archaeological Museum, Sofia.

Right: a bronze gladiatorial helmet from Pompeii. Museo Archeologico Nazionale, Naples.

space occupied by a large bear, lion or tiger would be 16 square palms, the area would be capable of containing 6,737 wild beasts. But, since not all wild beasts were the same size, then, calculating 10 square palms for each one, the arena could hold 10,779 beasts. The totals of 5,000 exhibited by Titus and of 9,000 displayed by Probus, are not exaggerated. Yet, let it be understood, not to have them all killed *uno die* in the Amphitheatre, but to show them all *uno die* to the people".

Those hundred inaugural days certainly cost a lot of money, but in comparison with how much the Emperor had invested in the building of the amphitheatre it was just small change; with the sum spent on the construction of the Colosseum "a capital city could have been constructed".

In those three months and more that followed the solemn ceremony in which the Emperor entrusted the new building to the care of the gods, there were shows not only in the Colosseum arena and 'in the wood of Caius and Lucius', but also in the ancient Naumachia of Augustus beyond the Tiber. There on the third day a naval battle was staged with the participation of three thousand men.

The inauguration of the building was commemorated by a coin issue, a bronze sesterce, representing on one face the Emperor, and on the other the Colosseum overflowing with spectators.

Domitian also loved the elliptical arena of the Colosseum, perhaps more at night, lit up by torches and trodden by women gladiators. We know that he was in the habit of entertaining in the royal box with a child (*puerulus*) dressed in scarlet (*coccinatus*) crouched at his feet.

The boy was maybe the eleven-year-old Q. Sulpicius Maximus, crowned on the Capitol by the same Emperor for having won a poetry competition; his sepulchre was found when the right-hand tower of the Salaria Gate was demolished in 1871.

It was Domitian who had the amphitheatre arena fitted out to represent the myth of Orpheus: there were the mountain and the Hesperides' garden where Orpheus sang, while all around trees and rocks were filled with every kind of animal and bird; acrobat boys rode bulls grasping them by the horns while Orpheus, impersonated by a criminal, was rent apart by a bear. Martial was the official poet to whom was given the task of describing the shows under the Flavians in the Colosseum; "a woman", says the poet, "overcame and killed a lion. One of the most hardened outlaws was crucified and exposed not to a false bear, like the actor and mimic Laureulus in the play of Naevius, but to a real Caledonian bear, which tore him into pieces. A condemned man, who like Daedalus had to fly to escape the claws of a bear, fell to earth, and was lacerated by the beast. A rhinoceros tossed a lion around with its horn. A lion that had wounded his master or tamer was killed with arrows by order of the Emperor. A bear,

which had to defend itself from the blows of the bestiary, covered its head with its forepaws and rolled away to escape from the bloody arena; but it was forced to stop, caught in a trap like a bird. Bestiary Carpophorus deserved to be preferred to Meleager and to Hercules, since in the same day and in the same show he killed 20 wild beasts: among them two heifers, a buffalo, a bison, a bear and a lion of great size, together with a very fast leopard. A machine raised a bull high in the middle of the arena; on its back had been placed the image of Domitian disguised as Hercules. Such machines were constructed in the workshop *summum choragium*. They were put together with such skill, that by themselves they elevated their various concealed platforms. Moreover, they changed shape, unwinding the parts which were joined together, reuniting those spread out, or slowly lowering those elevated. Sometimes they featured gladiators, pleasant fires and other surprises of this kind. An elephant, having killed a bull, knelt down in front of Domitian; a tiger succeeded in seriously wounding a lion (a new event, which had never occurred before) and a bull which, excited by the flames all over the arena, had thrown into the air many puppets, *pilae*, was killed at last by an elephant, that in its turn tossed the bull about with its trunk".

Trajan also loved the *ludi* and put on some wonderful shows in the Colosseum. For his triumph over the Dacians he had 10,000 gladiators and 11,000 wild beasts fight there. Hadrian, when he was in Rome, not only attended the shows but also descended into the arena to kill personally some wild beasts. During the games he offered, as did Titus before him, globes with gifts inside for the spectators. Antoninus Pius wanted to amaze the Romans by preparing hunts with the participation of animals coming from the most remote areas of the world, such as crocodiles, hippopotamuses, gazelles, hyaenas.

Marcus Aurelius did not demonstrate interest in any kind of show, though he participated in them so as not to rouse the people's discontent. During the *ludi* he used to write and to give audiences, as Julius Caesar had done. However, Marcus Aurelius enlisted many gladiators in the war against the Marcomanni, and in just one show in the Colosseum he had a hundred lions killed.

The profession of gladiator during the reign of Commodus was modified by law from 'infamous' to 'noble', with the result that the *Collegium Silvanum Aurelianum* was formed, composed of four *decuriae*. At their disposal was a temple dedicated to the gladiators' god Silvanus. Very probably in the same period the College of Bestiaries, mentioned on a tablet, was instituted.

These transformations were not fortuitous; no Roman emperor loved amphitheatrical shows more than Commodus; in fact he himself was a very good gladiator. When the emperor went into the arena the terraces were unbelievably packed, since the spectators came from every part of Italy to support that 'god-gladiator' who killed so many wild beasts and won so many fights. He entered the arena 635 times and overcame one thousand gladiators. He attended Rome's great barracks (*Ludus Magnus*) assiduously; in the stretch of road that led to the amphitheatre he dressed as Hercules with a club in his hands and a lion

skin on his body. He often attended the games dressed as an amazon or a woman, and against every custom he ordered that the spectators should wear the loose gown (*paenula*) as they did on occasion of funerals.

On one occasion, having beheaded an ostrich with his sword in the arena, Commodus approached some senators, among them Cassius Dion who has handed down to us this fact; with a menacing and provocative air he held up in his right hand the bloody sword and in his left the bird's head, as a warning that the same thing would be done to them. Commodus was the son of Faustina, wife of Marcus Aurelius, and maybe of a gladiator. In the shows they conferred on him the title of *Palus primus Secutorum*. He lived and behaved like any slave -fighter, drinking and cursing; but, unlike "real" gladiators who entered the arena for a few coins, he, as Dion says, "was content every day with one million of sesterces".

Septimus Severus, to celebrate the first ten years of his reign, gave several shows in the Colosseum; a singular one amongst these was that of a ship containing 400 wild animals, which were allowed out one at a time. Caracalla delighted both in watching the *ludi* and *venationes* and in personally venturing into the arena: he killed a tiger and an elephant with his own hands. In one show he compelled the popular gladiator Batone to fight three times in the same day, but his tiredness was fatal and finally he was killed. The Emperor honoured the athlete's corpse with splendid obsequies and built for him on the via Aurelia a sepulcre which, besides the inscription BA.TO.NI., bore engraved the figure of the gladiator with bands bound around his chest. In 217 A.D. under the rule of Macrinus,

the amphitheatre was damaged by a fire provoked by lightning; as a result the gladiatorial games were suspended for a while. Elagabalus nourished a real passion for the *venationes* and in particular for the animals. Aelius Lampridius narrates that once the Emperor did not leave the amphitheatre even to have lunch; he had his table prepared on the highest point of the edifice. Alexander Severus struck a medal in 223 A.D. on which is represented a fight between a *venator* and a wild beast in the Colosseum arena; outside, the Emperor is seen on the point of entering the building followed by a guard.

Gordian III had held unprecedented games in order to celebrate his Persian triumph. In Rome there were already 22 elephants, 60 lions, 10 tigers, 10 elk , 10 hyaenas, 1 hippopotamus, 1 rhinoceros, 10 camels, 40 wild horses, 20 onagers, in addition to 1,000 pairs of gladiators. Beasts and athletes were used by his murderer and successor Philip the Arabian when on 21st April 248 A.D. he celebrated the millenium of the foundation of Rome with the *Ludi Saeculares*. Actually, historians do not agree about the site where these *ludi* took place, whether in the Colosseum, in the Circus Maximus or in the Theatre of Pompey. As we are sure that the Emperor distributed gifts to the spectators, it would follow that the games were performed in the amphitheatre, a place traditionally 'reserved' for this, but it is probable, however, that the *Ludi Saeculares* were celebrated in several arenas of the city.

Gallienus was a man of great wit; it was said that, on his wife's insistence, he once punished a man who had sold her some fake jewels. The Emperor ordered the swindler to be thrown into the arena as a meal for the lions; but, at

Unlike gladiatorial combat, which was banned in the fifth century, the venationes continued until the reign of Teodorico. The last such event was held under his auspices in 523 A.D. The bestiarii or hunters usually had to face wild animals such as tigers, lions, bears, boars and hyenas. Occasionally they had the good fortune to encounter less threatening animals, such as giraffes, deer and ostriches.
Below: a fourth century floor mosaic depicting the capture of a boar. This forms part of the famous Piazza Armerina mosaics in Sicily.

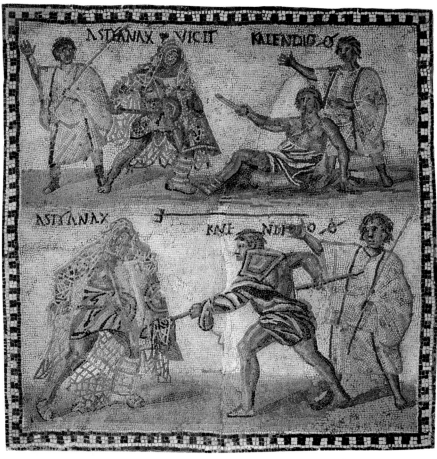

Right: scenes of gladiatorial combat from a Roman mosaic of the fourth century. The scene also features two retiarii. These were the gladiators who fought with just a net, used for entrapping their opponents, and a trident, used for finishing them off. Museo Arqueológico Nacional, Madrid.

Below: a rather inaccurate artist's representation of the amphitheatre games in Colosseum in a naive print by Jacopo Lauro.

the crucial moment, from the hypogean trap-door there sprang out a capon. After the fright and the deception, the man was freed. On another occasion a gladiator tried in vain ten times to kill a bull; the Emperor's response was to crown him. Gallienus replied to the protests of the public that the prize was deserved, since it was a difficult task not to be able to slaughter a bull with so many blows.

In 274 A.D., Aurelianus, pacifier of the Empire, triumphally celebrated in the city his victory over Palmyra. Forming part of the very rich eastern spoils were 800 pair of gladiators, many prisoners and various kinds of animals including 20 elephants; the triumph was honoured by games of every type, *ludi, venationes*, races in the circus, *naumachiae* and the ascent to the Capitol of Queen Zenobia bound in golden chains.

"Scenographic" games took place in the Colosseum during the times of Caro (282-283) and Numerianus and Carinus (283-284), which were described by Calpurnius in the *Egloga VII*. He has the shepherd Coridon, as an eyewitness, outlining the shows given in the Flavian Amphitheatre.

Diocletian refused to organize shows and harshly criticized the expenditure of his precedessors for this purpose. The first Christian Emperor, Constantine, issued a law in 325 A.D. universally forbidding gladiatorial performances.

Already ten years before the Emperor had abolished the cruel habit of branding condemned gladiators on their foreheads with red-hot iron. Moreover, he drew up a further law forbidding the judges to sentence criminals to gladiatorial service, replacing this punishment with forced labour in the mines. The stubborn struggle carried on by Constantine and by the nascent Christian civilization against gladiatorial games was beginning to bear fruit; but in the Flavian Amphitheatre shows continued to be performed, because of the great passion the Romans nourished for them. To stop them would have been imprudent indeed. We have a witness in the person of Alipius, reported by St. Augustine, who reveals that in 390 A.D., in the reigns of Theodosius I and Valentinian II games were performed in the Colosseum. Alipius was a Christian baptized in Milan by St. Ambrose. Forced by some friends to attend a spectacle in the Flavian Amphitheatre, he tried to keep his eyes closed, but when, after a remarkable blow by a gladiator, the spectators jumped to their feet acclaiming him loudly, Alipius was won over by curiosity and opened his eyes; he found himself strongly attracted by the sight of blood. Saint Augustine knew the 'danger' of the arena, its fascination and the importance it had for the Roman State: therefore he tried to keep Christians uncontaminated by its influence. The arena was the fulcrum of popular ritual, and brought heathen gods to the urban masses of the Empire. With its liturgy, its sacrifices, its hysteria and the presence of the images of the pagan gods and even of the deified Emperor, it represented for the first Christians a sort of devil's abode, the seat of the Antichrist.

In 357 A.D. Emperor Constance gave some instructions which adversely affected the organization of the shows: he forbade those who held a palatine rank to become gladiators and ordered the *munerarii*, under pain of a fine of six pounds of gold, not to entice the soldiers with money. In 397 A.D. Honorius stopped the senators having gladiators in their service, yet the *ludi* went on being performed in the amphitheatre under his reign, as Prudentius has testified. In 399 A.D., to celebrate and solemnize the consulate of Flavius Manlius Theodorus, hunts took place in the Colosseum. Still in the reign of Honorius, in 403 A.D. or in 404 A.D. a monk named Telemachus left the East for Rome with the intention of having the shows in the Colosseum stopped. During a fight he entered the arena and tried to speak to the spectators, who murdered him cruelly. The sacrifice of the monk's life pushed the Emperor towards abolishing these games for ever. Yet he let the *venationes* survive; they continued to be celebrated in the Flavian Amphitheatre until the sixth century. The reasons for this imperial decision can be found either in the fact that the people still had a strong interest in the arena and thus it would have been politically unwise to cancel the shows altogether, or that criminals were executed during the *venationes*. Not only according to the Emperor, but also to the condemned themselves, it was a humanitarian gesture for a person to be executed by a beast instead of by the hand of another man.

In 523 A.D., when Anicius Maximus became consul, the last performances of which we have record took place in the Colosseum. In a letter that Theodoric sent to consul Maximus, the king recommended compensating the *venatores* generously, and to prize them more than the singers, the instrument players and the wrestlers, because they were exposed to the ferocity of wild beasts. Theodoric's attitude is nevertheless ambiguous, in the way he concludes his letter: "Ah how lamentable are the errors of man! If there was but a faint flame of justice, such riches would be used in favour of men's lives, rather than thrown away in procuring their deaths".

SUGGESTED ITINERARY

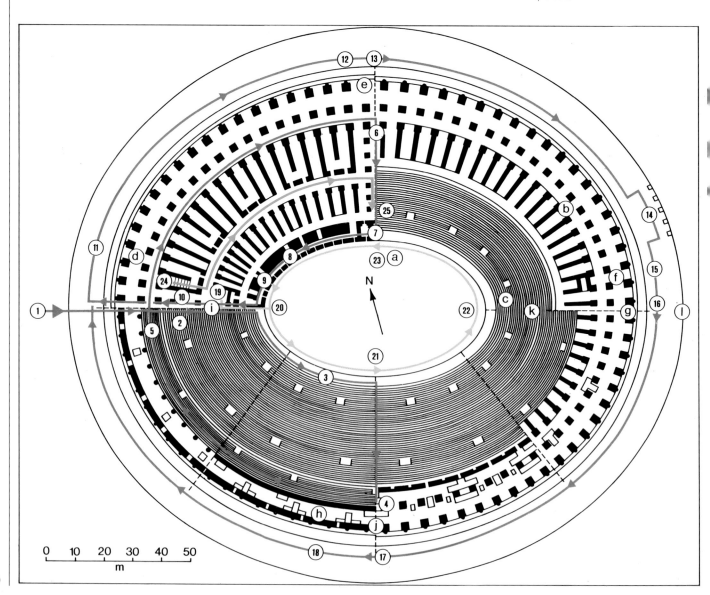

0 10 20 30 40 50
m

OTHER
AMPHITHEATRES
IN
THE ROMAN WORLD

THE POMPEII AMPHITHEATRE

«Caius Quinctius Valgus, son of Caius, and Marcus Porcius, son of Marcus, quinquennial duumviri, in recognition of the office bestowed on them, had built at their own expense this entertainment building and presented it to the citizens in perpetuity». This epigraph, engraved on a travertine slab and preserved in two copies, constituted the official dedication by which the quinquennial duumviri of the colony of Cornelia Veneria Pompeianorum donated to the citizens the fabric wholly erected at their own expense. Without doubt there exists no other amphitheatre preserved in such good condition, and none more ancient, as is witnessed by building techniques and by the fact that it was given the name of *spectacula*. The name *amphitheatrum* (i.e. a theatre with gradins all round) was not yet widespread; it was present in Vitruvian literature from the Augustinian era. The monument stood in the outskirts near the eastern corner of the town walls against which it leant. Thus the embankment was raised only on the side opposite the walls, using the earth coming from the excavation of the arena (at a difference in height of six metres compared with the roadway level of adjacent sites). In this way it was possible to avoid building more than one half of the containing scarp wall. On the counterforts of the outer wall were laid some semi-circular arches, linked together by a projecting cornice, making an exact ring on which rested the parapet of the outer higher ambulatory. The latter was a wide open-air passage, turning on the higher part of the amphitheatre drum; it could be reached by two large external staircases with two flights each and by two others with only one flight. Some painted inscriptions, now no longer legible, testified that on the days of the spectacles and by authority received from the *aediles,* the spaces under the external arches were occupied by pedlars of every kind.

Two wide corridors, entirely hollowed out of the embankment and slightly sloping inwards, permitted entrance into the arena, which could contain about twenty thousand spectators. The first one, rectilinear, opened northwards in line with the main axis, and was the main entrance. The vault was seriously damaged by the earthquake of 63 A.D., as is shown by brick restorations almost everywhere in the amphitheatre. The second corridor entered the arena from the opposite side of the main axis to the south, but it was less important since it bent sharply towards the eastern part of the monument. Near its opening onto the arena there were two narrow rooms at the sides; they were probably used as *spoliarium* to shelter the gladiators killed or wounded in the fights.

The cavea was subdivided into three horizontal orders: the *prima cavea,* close to the arena, the *media* and the *summa cavea*. This last, made up of eighteen rows of steps, was crowned by the baldric, that is the higher part of the building ending with the boxes, on the outer side of which, inside the higher passage, were inserted two rows of large stone rings intended to receive the poles of the *velarium*.

The wall of the podium separated the arena from the *prima cavea* and served as a parapet to a narrow passage close to the first rows of seats. Originally it was 2.18 m high and was decorated with wonderful paintings now lost, undoubtedly forming the most important ornament of the whole amphitheatre. The podium was adorned with scenes of gladiatorial fights or of hunts, spaced by Victories or by other surrounding elements.

A *crypta* under the cavea allowed quick entrance and exit of the spectators during performances. It was formed by four wings leading to the two main axis corridors which divided the amphitheatre into its western and eastern halves. It was also possible to reach these vaulted corridors through two other straight passages, whose entrances were on the western side of the monument to the right and to the left respectively of the large two-flight stair on the minor axis. Under this stair ran another straight corridor which gave access to the *prima cavea,* just before opening onto the arena. Here was the *pulvinar,* with its own entrance, reserved for the most eminent personages of the town. It communicated with the arena through a little door, which can be explained by the fact that victorious gladiators were allowed to enter the loggia to receive grace or proper acknowledgment from the duumviri or from their representatives. On the side opposite the *pulvinar* was the seat of the *rector spectaculi,* who superintended the games.

As for the drainage system, an indication is given by the shape of the cavea itself, whose steps, lowered at the rear, directed rainwater towards those of the wedges, which in turn carried it to the lower flights and from there, through suitable pipings, under the *prima cavea*. A small drain-pipe went right around the inner ambulatory, while water falling on the arena was absorbed by the embankment. That flowing onto the higher outer ambulatory was conveyed to the square by way of the staircases.

The lack of hypogea, necessary to the staging of games with animals and with large scenery, indicates that in the arena mostly gladiatorial *ludi* were performed. In fact, amphitheatres originated principally for such spectacles and not for *venationes* which spread only in the Julio-Claudian period and caused a real transformation in amphitheatre structure.

Left: a fresco from Pompeii showing the amphitheatre. The scene shows an episode from the reign of Nero when fighting broke out between the residents of Pompeii and those of nearby Nuceria, who had come to Pompeii for the gladiatorial games.

Below: the remains of the oldest known amphitheatre, namely that of Pompeii, built in the first century B.C. The cavea is divided into three levels, the lowest of which is separated from the arena by the podium wall.

THE NIMES AMPHITHEATRE

The city of Nîmes (*Nemausus*) in *Gallia Narbonensis* is still today called the 'French Rome' for the numerous Roman monuments it preserves. The amphitheatre is among the most admired for its fine state of preservation and its wide dimensions: 133 × 101 m the axes of the outer ellipse, 69 × 38 m the axes of the arena, 21 m the height of the outer prospect.

In the outer wall, constructed in big parallelepiped limestone blocks squared and connected without cramps, there are sixty arches framed by two Doric orders and surmounted by an attic. The four principal barrel-vaults at the extremities of the two main axes are slightly wider and jut out, serving as gates. The *Porta Triumphalis* and the *Libitinensis* are on the longer axis; on the minor axis the entrances to the boxes of the authorities were decorated with two columns surmounted by a gable with a bull-shaped protome in relief, a motif that can be found also on the higher order. From a structural point of view, the building is conceived with load-bearing elements made of the same limestone as the façade; secondary elements of square tiles of the same stone, laid down and cemented; vaults built with radial blocks, disposed like wedges and bound by mortar.

In the higher part of the attic some corbels were set, furnished with a hole through which passed the pole (*malus*), whose lower extremity fitted into the cornice below. Inside, in correspondence with the pierced corbels, another series of supports housed other poles and the cross-pieces strengthening them. As in the Colosseum, to these *mali* were fastened the ropes tightening the gores of the *velarium*. Behind the order of the attic, a low barrel-vaulted corridor, besides serving the *velarium*, had to light the wall of the attic itself.

Every second arch, a passage from the outer gallery on the ground floor led to the inner gallery; this passage alternated with a stair climbing to the upper floor, where the access stairs to the *vomitoria* in the cavea were situated. Stairs and walkways connected the first circle with the second; starting from the inner gallery, and the third with the fourth from the gallery of the higher floor; above this gallery another corridor formed the *summa cavea*. In total, the amphitheatre could contain up to 24,000 spectators.

Right: the amphitheatre of Nimes, which was built in the first century A.D. The building, which has two orders of arches and was originally surmounted by an attic, is in good condition and is still used for bullfights and other shows.

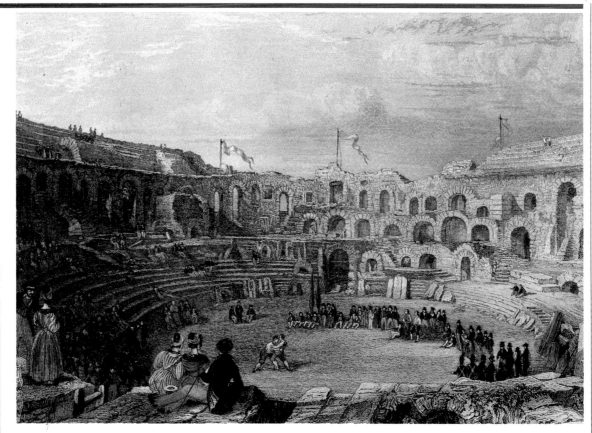

The arena rests on a natural layer, except in the central part, where two underground galleries six m wide, three m deep and 36 m long run under the minor and major axes, forming a cross. These galleries were originally covered with wood, set at the same level as the arena. The walls are of small parallelepipedal limestone ashlars and still show the cavities which housed the poles supporting the boards. Two identical inscriptions in shallow uncial letters, *T. Crispius Reburrus fecit*, almost certainly reveal who constructed the underdground room in a period following the building of the monument. This period is thought to be in the years between Domitian and Trajan. Building details were very well executed. For example, in order to impede currents of air, the *vomitoria* have not been placed in the continuation of the corridors; also, to avoid crowding the spectators, the stairs widen downwards.

The drainage system for rainwater is a masterpiece of plumbing. All gradins are slightly inclined towards the centre of the arena, conveying water to the four big collecting gutters. One gutter is in the gallery of the first *maenianum* for water from the upper sector of the cavea; another is in the ground floor gallery for water from the lower section; a third is outside the fabric for the drainage of the roof gutters and a fourth leads all around the ellipse of the arena (*euripus*).
Rough bas-relief sculptures, were executed by local craftsmen.
At the northern entrance, which was the main one (*Porta Triumphalis*) since it faced the city, a relief in a pilaster of the she-wolf with the twins recalled the origin of the Roman stock and of the Caesarean dynasty.
Transformed into a fortress in the Middle Ages, the amphitheatre was restored in the last century; it is still used for bullfights and other shows.

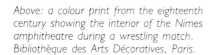

Above: a colour print from the eighteenth century showing the interior of the Nimes amphitheatre during a wrestling match. Bibliothèque des Arts Décoratives, Paris.

THE ARLES AMPHITHEATRE

This is the largest Roman amphitheatre in France with axes of 136 × 107 m and two outer orders, Doric below and Corinthian above, framing sixty arches of 3.50 m average width. It was built close to the ramparts of a rocky spur overlooking the town, near the ancient first century B.C. theatre, the Romanesque cathedral of St. Trophime and the little church of Nôtre-Dame-la-Major.
Its dating is a strongly debated matter; nowadays most scholars incline towards the first century A.D., the period from the reign of Nero to that of Vespasian in particular.
The cavea has a 34° slope and all its structures are of brickwork, partly *opus caementicium* and partly *opus quadratum*, including the *maenianum summum*, which was made of wood in the Colosseum. There were four series of steps every *maenianum*, separated by the precincts;

the first four steps were reserved for persons of consequence. Up to 26,000 spectators could be seated.
On the podium some leaning slabs bore a long inscription (about 10.30 m) dating back to the end of the first or to the beginning of the second century A.D. These stated that the flamen (maybe Augustalis) Caius Junius Priscus, to celebrate his five-year appointment as duumvir of Arles, took care of the building of the podium with the gates by supplementing considerably from his own resources the sum placed at his disposal by the authorities of the colony. He also placed there two silver statues of Neptune. Furthermore, he paid for some *venationes* and had special seats installed in the first *maenianum* for some of the magistrates, among whom were, according to custom, the *Navicularii* and the *Seviri Augustales*. It is likely that the inscription refers not to the first building of the podium but to a

restoration or, better, to a renewal financed by Priscus on the occasion of his appointment.
The arena is almost entirely dug out of the rock in a hollow between two hills. About three m under the edge of the podium parapet the paving was laid; it consisted of wooden boards supported by a beam framework. The real arena floor was 5.20 m below the same point of reference. Thus the provision of a double partly movable floor created space for storing equipment, material and beasts. In addition, it made cleaning easier and allowed the arena to be used even when the base was flooded. Such deposits of water were carried away by a cuniculus which led to the valley.
In the Middle Ages the amphitheatre was transformed into a fortified redoubt by the erection of three towers on the upper level (XIII century). Reconstructed in some sections, it is used today for bull-fights.

The amphitheatre of Arles was built during the Flavian period. It is a monumental structure dug out of the rock in the incline between two hills. The cavea, whose brickwork is partially cemented, is exceptionally well preserved.

THE POLA AMPHITHEATRE

The town of Pola, nowadays lying in Yugoslavian territory near the south-western extremity of the Istrian peninsula, was once inside Italic territory, precisely in the *Regio X Italiae Augustea*, the *Venetia et Histria*. The wonderful state of conservation of the outer wall of white Istrian stone and the pleasant situation close to a hill overlooking the sea make of this amphitheatre one of the most evocative monuments of the Roman world. Though the outer ring of the building up to the attic survives almost intact, on the inside the original cavea and gradins are almost completely missing. There remain only radial walls. In the eastern part near the hill, a section of the gradins has been rebuilt, to allow theatrical performances to take place. The external frontage is 30.45 m high and the axes are 132 × 105 m long (a ratio of 1:26). The whole structure is thought to have been able to contain 23,000 spectators when full. Such a figure, higher than that of the inhabitants of the town, shows that people living in the country flocked from every part of the hinterland when *ludi* were performed.

The morphological situation of the site heavily conditioned the erection of the building. On the side facing the sea it is possible to note a mighty architraved base functioning as support, on which rest two orders of arches (72 in all), stressed by Tuscan pillars framed by pilaster strips. The third order is formed by a circular attic in which are situated quadrangular windows. On the eastern side, however, the first order and the supporting base are completely absent; the hill takes over their function. Every order is stressed by cornices. The arch lintels are based on corbels, interrupted by pilaster strips on the outer side, in the central part of the pilasters. The last projecting cornice, over the windows of the attic, is surmounted by a line of open-work eaves - well preserved at some points - on which lay the wooden beam-work intended to support the *velarium*.

One of the most remarkable characteristics is the presence of four towers whose foreparts project outside the walls, not in correspondance with the ellipse axes but at the centre of the respective quadrants.

All of them were furnished with two inner stairs that permitted access up to the attic; the outer windows still show in some places the transenna stone decoration imitating the wooden beam-work. It is very probable that tanks storing water were housed on the top of the towers in order to feed fountains and scenic games. The north-western tower is the best preserved.

The cavea was divided into two main *maeniana* separated by a corridor. Illustrious personages and guests of honour were seated in the boxes of honour, set in the centre of the long sides, and in the podium which was the nearest section to the arena. Under the podium there was a series of service rooms for the gladiators, including the *Portae Posticiae*, through which they could all of a sudden enter the arena or take shelter from the beasts.

The arena was provided with underground structures, to support the wooden floor, only from the Flavian era. With the addition of this structure, which was reached by a tunnel from the west side, the performance of aquatic shows and *naumachiae* was no longer possible.

The front of the outer ring of the amphitheatre of Pola. The arches are supported by Tuscan pillars and framed by pilaster strips. Here we see one of the four jutting avant-corps, positioned on the axes of the ellipse. Each of these housed two internal staircases which provided access to the attic.

THE AMPHITHEATRES IN THE ROMAN WORLD

1 Alba Fucens, I A.D
2 Albano, III A.D.
3 Albingaunum (Albenga), II A.D.
4 Ancona, I B.C.-I A.D.
5 Ariminum, I A.D.
6 Arretium (Arezzo), I-II A.D.
7 Augusta Bagiennorum (Benevagienna), I-II A.D.
8 Augusta Praetoria (Aosta), I B.C. - I A.D.
9 Capua, I-II A.D.
10 Caralis (Cagliari), II A.D.
11 Casinum (Cassino), I A.D.
12 Catana, I A.D.
13 Forum Cornelii (Imola), I A.D.
14 Interamnia (Teramo), I A.D.
15 Libarna (Serravalle Scrivia), I-II A.D.
16 Luceria, I B.C. - I A.D.
17 Luna (Luni), II A.D.
18 Lupiae (Lecce), II A.D.

19 Mediolanum, I-II A.D.
20 Pola, I A.D.
21 Pompeii, I B.C.
22 Puteoli (Pozzuoli), I A.D.
23 Rome Flavian Amphitheatre, I A.D.
   Castrense Amphitheatre, III A.D.
24 Spoletium, II A.D.
25 Sutrium, I B.C.
26 Syracusae, I B.C.
27 Thermae Himereae, I B.C. - I A.D.
28 Tusculum, II A.D.
29 Velleia, I A.D.
30 Venusia, I A.D.
31 Verona, I A.D.
32 Leptis Magna, I A.D.
33 Sabratha, II A.D.
34 Thysdrus (El-Djem), III A.D.
35 Tipasa, III A.D.
36 Augusta Emerita (Merida), I B.C.
37 Italica, I A.D.

38 Tarraco (Tarragona), I A.D. (?)
39 Arelate (Arles), I A.D.
40 Augusta Treverorum (Treviri), II A.D.
41 Augustoritum (Limoges), II A.D.
42 Burdigala (Bordeaux), III A.D.
43 Cemenelum (Cimiez), I-III A.D.
44 Forum Iulii (Frejus), I A.D.
45 Limonum Pictonum (Poitiers), II A.D. (?)
46 Lugdunum (Lione), I A.D.
47 Mediolanium Santonum (Saintes), I A.D.
48 Nemausus (Nimes), I A.D.
49 Segusio (Susa), III A.D.
50 Vesunna (Perigueux), I A.D.
51 Aventicum (Avenches), I A.D. (?)
52 Vindonissa (Windisch), I A.D.
53 Aquincum (Budapest), II A.D. (?)
54 Carnuntum (Petronell), III A.D. (?)
55 Salonae, II A.D.
56 Corinthus, III A.D.
57 Cyzicus, II A.D.

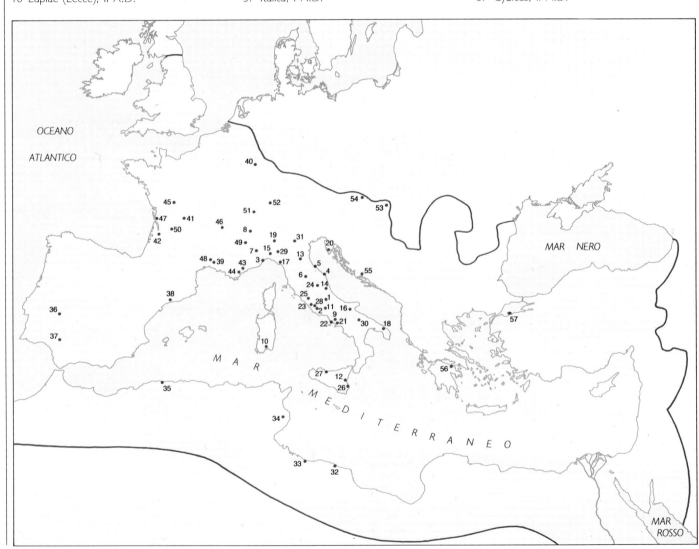

The photographs in this volume were provided by:
Archivio IGDA: 1, 8b, 35d, 41, 50b, 68b; S. Baiocco/P. Barontini: 15 a; Berengo Gardin: 77; M. Bizzicari: 36; J. Ciganovic: 17a; A. Dagli Orti: 15b, 40-41, 59, 64, 65; G. Dagli Orti: 7 a-b, 57, 67, 75, 76 a-b; A. De Antonis: 6, 9; C. Mocchegiani: 22 a-b-c; G. Nimatallah: 10-11 b, 14, 19, 23 a-b, 25, 26, 27 a-b, 28 b-c-d, 29, 30 a-b-c, 33 a-b, 34 a-b, 35 b-c, 38 a-d, 49 c, 50 a, 54, 55 a-b, 58, 68 a; Parker: 49 a; R. Pedicini: 73 a; Pubbliaerfoto: 2, 17 b, 74; Scala: 60-61, 62-63; Soprinten-denza Archeologica di Roma: 10-11 a, 12, 12-13, 20-21, 21 a-b, 24, 34 c; Studio Bellisario-Müller: 17 b, 37, 38 b; A. Vergani: 73 b; G. Zander: 8 a.